THE UNIVERSITY COLLEGE OF RIPON AND YORK ST. JOHN

Chicanc ... ; of
literary ... hat
forms t ... eals
how a ... ng-
ing fro ... e la
Cruz to ... ipe
Herrer ... nd
the stor ... om
Bernal ... nal
space a ... l as
factors ... ing
from c ... az.
Heterc ... :ed
and the ... ce.

Please return this book by the date stamped below
if recalled, the loan is reduced to 10 days

CANCELLED
1 JUN 1999

- 3 FEB 2000

23 MAY 2000

RETURNED

17 JUN 2010

13 MAY 2023

WITHDRAWN

Fines are payable for late ret—

D1330689

156068

College of Ripon & York St. John

3 8025 00363726 4

Chicano Poetics

CAMBRIDGE STUDIES IN AMERICAN LITERATURE AND CULTURE

Editor

Eric Sundquist, *University of California, Los Angeles*

Founding Editor

Albert Gelpi, *Stanford University*

Advisory Board

Nina Baym, *University of Illinois, Urbana–Champaign*
Sacvan Bercovitch, *Harvard University*
Albert Gelpi, *Stanford University*
Myra Jehlen, *Rutgers University*
Carolyn Porter, *University of California, Berkeley*
Robert Stepto, *Yale University*
Tony Tanner, *King's College, Cambridge University*

(Series listing continued following index)

Chicano Poetics

HETEROTEXTS AND HYBRIDITIES

Alfred Arteaga
University of California, Berkeley

CAMBRIDGE
UNIVERSITY PRESS

PUBLISHED BY THE PRESS SYNDICATE OF THE UNIVERSITY OF CAMBRIDGE
The Pitt Building, Trumpington Street, Cambridge CB2 1RP

CAMBRIDGE UNIVERSITY PRESS
The Edinburgh Building, Cambridge CB2 2RU, United Kingdom
40 West 20th Street, New York, NY 10111–3211, USA
10 Stamford Road, Oakleigh, Melbourne 3166, Australia

© Cambridge University Press 1997

This book is in copyright. Subject to statutory exception
and to the provisions of relevant collective licensing agreements,
no reproduction of any part may take place without
the written permission of Cambridge University Press.

First published 1997

Printed in the United States of America

Typeset in Bembo

*A catalogue record for this book is available from
the British Library*

Library of Congress Cataloguing-in-Publication Data
Arteaga, Alfred, 1950–
Chicano poetics : heterotexts and hybridities / Alfred Arteaga.
p.   cm. – (Cambridge studies in American literature and culture)
Includes bibliographical references and index.
ISBN 0-521-57370-X (hb). – ISBN 0-521-57492-7 (pb)
1. American literature – Mexican American authors – History and
criticism – Theory, etc.   2. Literature and society – United States.
3. Mexican Americans in literature.   I. Title.   II. Series.
PS153.M4A77   1997
810.9'86672–dc21   97-12730
                                                        CIP

ISBN 0 521 57370-X hardback
ISBN 0 521 57492-7 paperback

para
Xóchitl,
hija mía

Contents

Acknowledgments

I wish to thank several poets for the use of their poetry, including Juan Felipe Herrera for "Your Name is X," Francisco X. Alarcón for "Banderas," and Alurista for "Pachuco Paz."

"Poema en tres idiomas y caló" from *Undocumented Love* by José Antonio Burciaga (1992) and "Canto Primero," "Respuesta a Frida," and "Small Sea of Europe" from *Cantos* by Alfred Arteaga (1991) are reprinted by permission of Chusma House Publications.

"Net Laguna" appeared in *Contextos,* by Juvenal Acosta, Alfred Arteaga, Mario Quintero, and Carmen Roselló (1994) and is reprinted by permission of Moving Parts Press.

"From Where We Sit Corpus Christi" and excerpts of "Poem for the Young White Man Who Asked Me How I, an Intelligent Well-Read Person Could Believe in the War Between Races" and "Visions of Mexico While at a Writing Symposium at Port Townsend, Washington" are from *Emplumada* by Lorna Dee Cervantes (1981) and reprinted by permission of the University of Pittsburgh Press.

"Tricks of Gender Xing" appeared in *Stanford Humanities Review* 3.1 (1993) and is reprinted by permission of the Stanford Humanities Review.

"An Other Tongue" appeared in *An Other Tongue: Nation and Ethnicity in the Linguistic Borderlands,* edited by Alfred Arteaga (1994) and is reprinted by permission of Duke University Press.

" 'Beasts and Jagged Strokes of Color': The Poetics of Hybridisation on the US-Mexican Border" appeared in *Bakhtin: Carnival and Other Subjects, Critical Studies* 3.2 and 4.1–2, edited by David Shepherd (1993) and is reprinted by permission of Editions Rodopi.

gracias to MXM in Co. Sligo

Chicano Poetics

Introduction

Canto Primero

Arrival

First, the island.
The cross of truth.
Another island.
A continent.
A line, half water, half metal.

An island of birds, "Ccollanan."
An island of birds,
"Ccollanan Pachacutec!"
Sounds above an island, in
the air, trees, "Ccollanan Pachacutec!"
Female sounds. "Ricuy
anceacunac yahuarniy richacaucuta!"
An island of female birds, imagine
the sounds, the air, the trees, at times
the silence, the slither in thorns.

So perfect a shape, right
angles, the globe yields to so
straight a line, look. One
line, zenith to nadir, heaven,
precipitation. The only other,
straighter still than that horizon
we see at sea, perfect: paradise.
That horizontal line, from

old to new, he knew would yield,
yes, so perfect a move, he
knew, yes, so perfect a shape
yes.

Trees caught his thoughts.
Birds and onshores brought them
from the boats. She knew those
thoughts, heard those songs.
Could there be one more island?
Birds, sounds, perhaps pearls,
gold? Eden-Guanahaní, perhaps
another? "O my Marina, my new
found island. License my roaving
hands, and let them go, before,
behind, between, above, below."
West.

América, América. Feminine
first name, continent named
for him. América.
Here, Santa Fe. Here, the true
faith. I claim, in the name of
the father. Land of thorns,
in the name of the son.

The edge of this world
and the other, is marked
in water: ocean, river, wave to
her, she waits on the other
side. Aquí, se llama la Juana,
de apellido Juárez, india,
prieta y chaparra, la que le encanta
al gringo, al gachupín.

Island of cactus, genus
Cuauhtémoc. Island of rose,
land of thorns. Pedro de

Alvarado, an eagle, la
región transparente, a
night of smoke. Marina
Nightear, an ocean contained
in one woman, as it was in
the beginning, world
without end, fallen
eagle.

So feminine a shape. So female
a bay. Another shape: gliding
birds. Another: touching trees.
True name of woman, Vera Cruz,
body of woman. "He named me
Xochitepec, yes so we are all flowers
of the mountain, all a woman's body,
that was one true thing he said in
his life." Above, birds,
leaves, above so woman a form.
Las quince letras: not the seven words:
Contestó Malintzin, "yes
I said yes I will Yes."

En el nombre
de la Virgen de las Espinas,
ella que en buen ora nasco,
this archeology is born: here
tibia, here ball courts, codices,
teeth. Inside, the caves are
painted. Here is an architecture,
see, toco, toco,
tocotín:

Tla ya timohuica,
totlazo Zuapilli,
maca ammo, Tonantzin,
titechemoilcahuíliz.

Mati itlatol ihiyo
Huel ni machicáhuac
no teco qui mati.

En la sangre, en las espinas
de la Virgen de Santa Fe,
these names are written:
América Estados-Unidos, née
México. I name her
Flower of the Mountain,
Coatepec-Cihuatepec-Cuicatepec
Amor Silvestre,
Terra Nova,
Cuerpo de Mujer.

The edge of this world
and the other, is marked
in metal: on this side America,
on this side América.
Nights they spill from
San Diego and Los Angeles
threading the steel mesh
como nada, los verdaderos
alambristas, buscando el cuerpo
de mujer, buscando,
Xochitepec.

Mestizaje/Difrasismo

How the Poem Means

Poets, I imagine, set themselves tasks when they undertake a book of poetry. These tasks must be bound up inextricably with authorial intention, aesthetic concerns, with the fact of poetry. And the poems themselves must be at least as varied as the poets, as the creators who write poems for reasons of ego, love, art, and perhaps even religion or politics. In some way the poem manifests the poet's task and yokes together the personal and the public of the craft, there where the voice of one touches others and multiplies.

I can speak for myself. When I wrote *Cantos*, I set to the task of working out poetically some sense of how one is Chicano. It was a personal matter and remains so, and the impulse to begin poetry there at the personal, at some point of me, makes sense. And yet it is just as truly a social matter, and the writing for other people makes just as much sense. I do not claim an exemplary life for anyone, do not claim possession of a purer piece of truth than anyone, but neither do I seek to erase the factors of time and place that coalesce as they do only in me. A poem is set into motion by my act, in all the particulars of my social and personal contexts, and it is set off outward to sing, to dance, to break bones, in the world beyond me.

But let me talk of the specific, of the point of departure for *Cantos*. I open the book with a point of particular significance to me, one that points to a larger issue for Chicanos and for Americans in general.[1] The first canto begins with the following stanza:

> First, the island.
> The cross of truth.

> Another island.
> A continent.
> A line, half water, half metal.

The last line, "A line, half water, half metal," seems to me, on the one hand, to point to the intersection of the personal and the social and, on the other, to point to something else.

Simply, that *line* signifies the border and a border not only in metaphor, but the actual physical and political borderline between the United States and Mexico, which is, after all, Rio Grande *water* from the Gulf of Mexico to El Paso and *metal* fence from there to the Pacific. The real borderline impinges upon me in real ways, figuring as a wedge in my family history and as a limit of Anglo tolerance for my kind. It is a line that crosses the personal and the social in me in profound ways.

It is the poetry of the expression that concerns me here. For one of the tasks I set for myself is to make poetry, to make something in language that does something. To evoke the border as "a line, half water, half metal" is not only to state a truth that bears at least some of the demands of logic, but to state a "truth" by means of a trope. *Cantos* can make a sense according to logic, but it also does the stuff of poetry, and in the first stanza, the troping of the borderline says something not only about the international demarcation, but something also about how language undertakes the act of being Chicano.

What I intended with that poetic line was to employ a poetic device of the preconquest Mexican Indian poets who wrote in Nahuatl, the language of the Aztecs. My attempt to evoke the border in a union of two elements, water and metal, was an attempt to employ a trope that was very characteristic of Nahuatl poetry and a general feature of Nahuatl language and thought. In *Llave del Náhuatl,* Angel María Garibay calls this trope *difrasismo.*[2] Difrasismo is the means of representing something in the coupling of two elements. In this way, city is *in atl in tepetl,* water and hill; body is *noma nocxi,* hand and feet. And perhaps the most well known difrasismo is that for poetry, *in xóchitl in cuicatl,* flower and song.

This coupling of elements, two to suggest another, reveals something of how poetry comes to mean in Nahuatl. Poets, such as Nezahualcoyotl, relied on this general tropic feature of Nahuatl, which, as Garibay observes, often conceives in binarisms.[3] To call body "hand and feet" is to conceive body by its parts, in effect, by synecdoche, the trope of the relation of part to whole. *Noma nocxi* does call to mind the single concept of the whole "body" from the parts "hand" and "feet," and as it does, it comes to mean according to the particular arrangement of the difrasismo, the Mexican two for one. In a slightly different figuration, *in atl in tepetl* signifies "city" as "water and hill." It is a difrasismo, as is *noma nocxi,* but water and hill are not related to city in the same manner as are hand and feet to body. Rather than parts for whole, perhaps the relationship is one of contiguity: water and hill signify city because they are near the city. This difrasismo is therefore one of metonymy. The term for poetry is more difficult. Flower and song is a difrasismo in which the two elements work differently. Song functions as a synonym, for Nahuatl poems were sung, that is, poems were songs. Flower, however, is a metaphor, for clearly flowers are not poems. *In xóchitl in cuicatl* is similar to the difrasismos for body and city in its significant coupling but different in the elements joined. Difrasismo pervades the Nahuatl language, so that the world is conceived by this common and multifaceted trope.[4]

I opened *Cantos* with a line that figured the border "half water, half metal," so as to locate my work in a relation to a Nahuatl world view. In one way, I employ the figure of thought merely to make reference to the Aztec perspective, to allude to an ancestral root of chicanismo. But in a more significant way, I put difrasismo to the task of signaling from the onset the character of thought in *Cantos,* in Chicano poetry, and in Chicano thought in general. Difrasismo seems to me a characteristic feature of how my poetry comes to meaning and of how one comes to being Chicano.

So while a poem seems to me a connection from the private to the public, *Cantos,* and Chicano poetry in general, seems to be able to make another sort of link. My attempt in "a line, half water, half metal" is to take an important concept for Chicanos, the border, and to articulate it in light of a mode of Mexican-Indian thought. To the degree that it calls to mind a sense of Indianness, it is similar in effect to what other Chicano poets do when they articulate Indianness. Examples range from Francisco Alarcón's translation and reworking of Nahuatl spells, to José Montoya's parody of identity politics, to Lorna Dee Cervantes's encounter with the god Mescalito and Gloria Anzaldúa's with the goddess Coatlicue.[5] In other words, it is common for Chicano poetry to mention something Indian. And in this way, allusion serves as a simple means of linking Chicano with the Indian element.

But the linking is more complex. The examples I chose, Alarcón, Montoya, Cervantes, and Anzaldúa, do much more than merely point to Indians. Each, in various ways, makes a statement about how the Indian presence affects the act of being Chicano. When Lorna Cervantes, in "Meeting Mescalito at Oak Hill Cemetery," and Gloria Anzaldúa, in "The *Coatlicue* State," cite Mexican deities, they introduce matters of alternate consciousness. Mescalito is the god of the hallucinogen peyote, and Coatlicue is the goddess of a feminine subjectivity. Their evocation serves to illustrate alternate possibilities for apprehending the world. Francisco Alarcón begins with a colonial translation of Nahuatl spells and makes *Snake Poems,* a collection of Chicano poetry. As he does, he weaves Aztec, as well as criollo, consciousness into contemporary Chicano thought. José Montoya parodies the politics of racial identity in "Hispanic Nightlife at Luna's Cafe When th' Mexicans Came to Visit th' Chicanos in Califas," dividing la raza into the Casindio, on the one hand, and Casispano, "also pronounced Cathipano," on the other. The work of these poets, in ways as disparate as the poets are themselves, asserts some link between Indian thought and Chicano identity, be it by parody or difrasismo.

This working out of Indianness as a factor in being Chicano is significant in the first instance because of historical fact. The border that is instanced in my poem or in Anzaldúa's book begins in Chicano consciousness as a real political fact, yet the factual border can be treated poetically, described as "capricious borders on the red continent," as "una herida abierta," or as the place where Chicanos wage *Undocumented Love.*[6] In other words, the border can be symbol and rendered poetic, but it is always a site of real world politics. It is not simply a metaphor.

The "reality" of the border for Chicanos is similar to the "reality" of the Indian. Consider for a moment the identity "Chicano" and the homeland "Aztlán." Chicano derives from Mexicano, which derives from Mexica, the name the Aztecs called themselves. "Chicano" recalls an older, original pronunciation. When Hernán Cortés conquered the Aztecs, the Spanish language still possessed the sound like the English "sh," represented in Spanish by the letter "x," so that the conquistador could approximate Meshica as Mexica. Eventually Spanish changed phonemically so that Meshico came to be pronounced Mehico (Méjico), and Don Quihote (Quijote), for another example, ceased to be Don Quishote (Quixote). The soft "ch" in Mexican Spanish approaches the "sh" of older Spanish and of Nahuatl, so that meshicano leads to mechicano and to chicano. In this manner, phonemically at least, Chicano signifies descent from the Aztecs. There is logic to this, for while Chicanos descend racially from many different Indians from Yucatán to California, the presence of the Aztec has been the most prominent in Mexican/Chicano culture.[7] The Chicano homeland, Aztlán, refers to the territories presently occupied by the United States but formerly part of Mexico, roughly, Texas to California. Aztlán is the mythical home of the Aztecs, from where they migrated south to central Mexico in 1168. To be a Chicano and to live in Aztlán is to have historical precedence over Anglos in the Southwest; it is to declare a historical fact of descent. The exact details of the fact are lost in the construction of a "national" identity, in the way national history is mythologized in the conception of any nation, but the general trajectory remains true: Chicanos descend historically from Indians.

But then after the facts of the border and of Indianness, there is the matter of how they are dealt with in the poetry. After the historical-political and historical-racial facts, the border and Indianness figure into the matter of Chicano subjectivity, into chicanismo, as sites and occasions of cultural interaction. The border is, after all, the line of national differentiation that gives birth to Chicanos, not just for having crossed it or having been crossed by it, but for living in the border zone between nations that the line engenders. Mexicans can transform into Chicanos on either side of the border, in Tijuana or Los Angeles, in Juárez or El Paso, and the border patrol hounds us as far as Chicago.

The border means that Chicano identity is constructed in defiance of the simple and absolute discretion of the state. To be Chicano in the borderlands is to make oneself from among the competing definitions of nation, culture, language, race, ethnicity, and so on.

As the border figures the Chicano in cultural difference, so Indianness figures the Chicano in racial difference. For while Chicano subjectivity comes about because of Anglo-American conquest of Northern Mexico, the Chicano body comes about because of *mestizaje*. And the original birth of that body comes about in the Spanish conquest of the Indians and in the raping of Indian women. From that violent colonial encounter, Mexican-Indians mixed with Spaniards to produce the hybrid race, the mestizo. The Indian is thus for the Chicano, the indigenous, the antecedent, the maternal half of our racial double helix. And like the border, Indianness is at once a site of origin and of cultural interaction. At each reproduction of the Chicano body, the racial characteristics of European and indigenous American compete for presence.

This use of the border and the Indian in Chicano poetry does something similar to that done by another feature. Linguistically, Chicano poetry often manifests some degree of interlingualism, employing English, Spanish, caló (Chicano slang), and perhaps Nahuatl.[8] In this way, the poems work out linguistically with thought what the border does culturally with the nation and what mestizaje does racially with the body. For good or for bad, this is the stuff of Chicano poetry: elements of difference interact in play and in competition within the parameters of chicanismo. This is as much as to say that the poetics of chicanismo are such that they locate the work of the poem in the working out of the individual, that an interlingual poem about border crossing or about Quetzalcoatl is a poem about hybridity, and that hybridity is the mode of both Chicano poem and Chicano subject.

Body, Place, Language

Let me continue by grounding my discussion of the poetics of Aztlán in the body, specifically in the racial body. The Mexican and Chicano are born in the colonial encounter between Europe and America. La raza did not exist before this, coming about only as a product of the violent and sexual encounter. The Chicano is racially hybrid, a mestizo, half European and half Indian. This configuration is accurate in the national mythology of Mexico and Aztlán and is founded on a historical fact: the first mestizos were the offspring of Spanish conquistadors and Indian women. But the reality of mestizaje is much more complex. For while the miscegenation had to begin in a one to one ratio, Spaniard male to Indian female, the subsequent course of the mestizaje was overwhelmingly Indian. And then there are the matters of what Indian, what European? Not all the Indians were Aztecs, for there is great diversity among indigenous people, including those the Aztecs thought racially different, such as the Mayans and the Tarascans. The Europeans too were diverse, since people other than Spaniards immigrated into Mexico, such as the French sent to impose Maximilian. Even the Spanish are a diverse people. And then of course Africans contributed to the gene pool, first as the slaves of the Spaniards, then as the runaway slaves of Anglo-Americans.

So what is the point of this, what does the racial hybridization mean? It means that the body, the physical manifestation of the Chicano, is itself a product of hybridity. Mestizaje means that the mestizo *is* the confluence of different races, in the senses of descending from an original hybrid begetting, of continually procreating mestizo offspring, and of simply being, in the present incarnation, multiracial. Hybridity is a fundamental physical reality of chicanismo. And a consequence of essential hybridity is subjective ambiguity. The mestizo can therefore be both indio and hispano: white Hispanic according to the U.S. census bureau and Indian according to relative composition of the gene pool. But the ambiguity is most significant not so much in the either/or racial binarism, that is, in not quite being either, as in the profound ambiguity of being both. For the body that is the product of diverse roots is more than the sum of those roots: there is something additional in being hybrid.[9]

The place *where* the mestizo body resides is also conceived ambiguously because of its own sort of hybridity. For Anglo-Americans, the Chicano lives in the United States, and with colonial amnesia, the

Chicano is conceived as an immigrant, an illegal border crosser whose home is a foreign nation south of the border. The convenient irony of this "Americanization" is that it affords Anglos precedence and preeminence in the Southwest, and it makes the "American" Chicano always deportable. This view is the inverse of the Mexican nationalist view that holds Chicanos as emigrants, and always returnable.[10]

Chicanos oppose the relatively facile national binarism in two different conceptions of Chicano space, Aztlán and the borderlands. While these concepts differ, they are similar in two aspects: both conceive Chicano space with a different logic than that which defines the traditional nation state, and accordingly both acknowledge states of overlapping identities. In other words, Aztlán and the borderlands are concepts of the homeland that do not directly parallel the concepts of nation as realized in the United States or Mexico, in part because Aztlán and the borderlands are more ambiguous than the territories of either nation state.

Aztlán is as old as Aztec mythology, but its contemporary use for Chicanos emerges from the cultural nationalist manifesto, El Plan Espiritual de Aztlán, written at the First Chicano National Conference in Denver in 1969 by the poet Alurista. The notion of the "plan" follows the tradition of Mexican revolution, during which revolutionary movements were launched with a plan named after the place where it was declared. The Aztlán plan begins:

> In the spirit of a new people that is conscious not only of its proud historical heritage but also of the brutal "gringo" invasion of our territories, *we,* the Chicano inhabitants and civilizers of the northern land of Aztlán from whence came our forefathers, reclaiming the land of their birth and consecrating the determination of our people of the sun, *declare* that the call of our blood is our power, our responsibility, and our inevitable destiny.
>
> We are free and sovereign to determine those tasks which are justly called for by our house, our land, the sweat of our brows, and by our hearts. Aztlán belongs to those who plant the seeds, water the fields, and gather the crops and not to the foreign Europeans. We do not recognize capricious frontiers on the bronze continents.

Brotherhood unites us, and love for our brothers makes us a people whose time has come and who struggles against the foreigner "gabacho" who exploits our riches and destroys our culture. With our heart in our hands and our hands in the soil, we declare the independence of our mestizo nation. We are a bronze people with a bronze culture. Before the world, before all of North America, before all our brothers in the bronze continent, we are a nation, we are a union of free pueblos, we are *Aztlán*.[11]

The plan declares a Chicano homeland, and in a move opposed to U.S. and Mexican nationalist perspectives, it renders the Chicano nondeportable. Aztlán is the home where Chicanos are indigenous; it is the land of forefathers and a gringo invasion. This declaration of the homeland responds to Anglo-American jingoism and xenophobia, to the calls in the 1960s for Chicanos and Mexicans to "Go back to Mexico," as well as to the current calls for their deportation and erasure. Because Aztlán is the original, northern homeland of the Aztecs, by virtue of ancestral presence and racial composition, the Chicano can envision "home" in territories now occupied by the U.S. nation state. This rhetoric of home reconfigures Anglo-Americans as " 'gringo,' " "foreign Europeans," and "foreigner 'gabacho.' " Point of view is reoriented so that what is the southwest from the perspective of Manifest Destiny becomes the "northern land" from the perspective of Mexico.[12] This simple change displaces Anglo America from the perspectival center and redefines the compass from a Mesoamerican center.

The plan also raises the question of nationalism. For while the declaration of Aztlán clearly asserts a cultural nationalism, it also enters into the discussion of nation, as a people and a state. "Mestizo nation," for example, can mean mestizo people, but the declaration of sovereignty and nation, "we are a nation, we are a union of free pueblos, we are *Aztlán*," locates that meaning within the parameters of the nation state. And the plan has it both ways, it is simultaneously *just* a cultural nationalist manifesto and a declaration of national independence. Where it asserts a nationalism of the state, it impinges upon international convention in general and upon the national definition of the United States in particular. For Aztlán is located within the political boundaries of the United States, and its declaration takes direct aim at Anglo-American hegemony. But because it is possible to view the plan as merely cultural nationalist, it is possible to wage anti-gringo rhetoric and yet avoid revolution. The conceived homeland is ambiguous enough to arouse passion, yet not mandate revolution.

The border, conceived as an amorphous area along the international borderline, is another figuration of Chicano space. Aztlán is defined as the territory taken by gringo invasion, that is, as land that was Mexico but is now part of the United States. The borderlands, too, are defined by the Anglo-American conquests, the annexation of Texas, the Mexican–American War, the Gadsen Purchase, but it is the fact of the borderline rather than acquisition of lands that organizes its space. Aztlán conceives Mexican immigration north as internal migration because Aztlán is the ancestral, Indian homeland. The borderlands emphasizes instead the facts of violence and cultural conflict within the interface between nations.

The two concepts are similar and both have informed the ideology of Chicano subjectivity. They differ, perhaps most significantly, in their ultimate telos. Aztlán aims at the homeland, at the nation as people, as state. It offers an interwoven history and myth of presence. It provides the principle of definition in the present and defines an idealized state in the future. As such it functions as the national myth in a manner similar to the myths of any people. The borderlands functions much less as a national telos. Perhaps its greatest use lies in conceptualizing relations of difference. Compared to Aztlán it is a poorer conception of homeland because one never knows where the real borderlands ends and the metaphoric one begins, when application of the term becomes merely symbolic appropriation.

The borderlands concept does not make the same claims to Indianness that Aztlán does.[13] That claim fosters the essentialist argument that Chicanos have more valuable presence in Aztlán than do Anglos in the Americas because Chicanos are more Indian. It is an argument well suited to conceiving the nation, Aztlán, homeland to Chicanos, descendants of the Aztecs. Instead, borderlands works against the tendency to define nation, for it emphasizes an overlap between nation states where the sharp distinctions are both contested and ambiguous.[14] One interesting consequence is that chicanismo need not exist only in the United States, for the border forces that shape lives in El Paso do so similarly in Juárez, in Los Angeles as in Tijuana. It is precisely this preoccupation with international forces and cultural conflict that so characterizes the notion of the borderlands.

So while Aztlán places relatively greater emphasis on the homeland, the borderlands emphasizes more the state of relations. As such, being Chicano is not so much to be resident of an area as to be subject to and to partake in the contestation of identities in that area. There, U.S. and Mexican identities, in their various manifestations, such as the national, the racial, and the linguistic, and every possible hybridization, compete for presence. There, identity is acted out within the matrices of political powers and cultural conflicts. This puts chicanismo at the site where social forces converge, and it stresses being Chicano as a dynamic of being in relation to others.

It is significant that the primary proponents of Aztlán and the borderlands have been, in both cases, poets. As Luis Leal points out:

> What interests us is not determining where Aztlán is found, but documenting the rebirth of the myth in Chicano thought. It is necessary to point out the fact that before March, 1969, the date of the Denver Conference, no one talked about Aztlán. In fact, the first time that it was mentioned in a Chicano document was in "El Plan Espiritual de Aztlán," which was presented in Denver at that time. Apparently, it owes its creation to the poet Alurista who already, during the Autumn of 1968, had spoken about Aztlán in a class for Chicanos held at San Diego State University.[15]

In 1987 Gloria Anzaldúa opened her book, *Borderlands/La Frontera: The New Mestiza,* with a now famous supplement to Alurista's concept. In "The Homeland, Aztlán/El otro México," she states: "The U.S.-Mexican border *es una herida abierta* where the Third World grates against the first and bleeds. And before a scab forms it hemorrhages again, the lifeblood of two worlds merging to form a third country – a border culture" (3).

That it is the poets who articulate the homeland and the national myth is no surprise, for this seems their proper function throughout the world. Consider David Lloyd's discussion of Ireland:

> Irish cultural nationalism has been preoccupied throughout its history with the possibility of producing a national genius who would at once speak for and forge a national identity. The national genius is to represent the nation in the double sense of depicting and embodying its spirit – or genius – as it is manifested in the changing forms of national life and history.[16]

Genaro Padilla takes this up in Aztec terms, describing Chicano poets (and other cultural workers) as *tlamatinime,* who create and transmit culture and who work the myths that bind a people.[17] Padilla also analyzes the relation of intellectual work to cultural nationalism in light of Franz Fanon's work on Algerian nationalism. In an early essay, "Franz Fanon and the National Culture of Aztlán," I undertake a similar strategy to explain the essential Indianness of Aztlán and the necessity of a progressive cultural production to define, and to maintain the presence of, a people.[18]

When Alurista and Gloria Anzaldúa speak of and forge the homeland, they do so in the language of that place. The language of Aztlán and the borderlands is a language of languages, not simply national language, like English or Spanish, but rather language as system. It is the site of confluence in the way the Chicano body is mestizo and the homeland is international. And like the body and home, the language is hybrid and thus more than merely a sum of its parts. Alurista and Anzaldúa write in a combination of English, Spanish, and the Chicano slang, caló. Both also introduce bits of the Nahuatl, which supplement the indigenous presence, the mexicanismos of Mexican Spanish. Chicano speech is like the mestizo body and the borderlands home: it simultaneously reflects multiple forces at play and asserts its hybridity.

When Gloria Anzaldúa writes lines like "This land was Mexican once, / was Indian always / and is. / And will be again. // Yo soy un puente tendido / del mundo gabacho al del mojado . . . ," she brings the border into her words (3). And when Alurista writes a poem like "Who are We? . . . Somos Aztlán: A Letter to 'El Jefe Corky,' " he brings the homeland into his words.[19] Both incorporate chicanismo not only as the object of the words but in the actual words themselves. The poems reflect Chicano speech and thought, for linguistic hybridization is the fact of Chicano articulation. In the manner that Alurista and Anzaldúa create the Chicano homeland in the consciousness by writing about it, they also create Chicano consciousness by writing in its terms. In other words, they serve the function of the national genius in the content and form of their work.

Language itself, the very fabric of the poem, is significant in the delineation of a homeland and its people. Poetic language is particularly suited to the task of myth, to envisioning a national origin, and to the tasks of defining a people, their place on the planet, and their future. For Chicano poets, Alurista, Anzaldúa, and the majority of the rest, language is hybrid. This caló, in its general sense of Chicano interlingual speech, defines a people as a national language defines a nation but not quite in the same way. It does not so thoroughly base subjectivity on a content, like the simple lexicon of a national language, as define the diverse cultural forces participating in the construction of a subjectivity. It speaks for and forges a hybrid people, a mestizo, borderland people who articulate in language the cultural conflicts in which they are enmeshed. The Chicano subject is not so much the subject of a language as the subject of language.

The interlingual speech of the Chicano and the hybridized poem in particular are especially apt at expressing the ambiguities inherent in mestizaje and those in either Aztlán or the borderlands. The Chicano's hybrid thought allows for a movement among discourses that replicates the possible range of perspectives on race or the homeland. This speech is interlingual in that it not only acknowledges a confluence of difference but emphasizes the factor of hybridity. It readily permits a fluidity in conceiving race and homeland by treating these concepts as categories of concepts that are composed of multiple and conflicting texts. Mestizaje is therefore not the simple and difficult problem it is for racial purists, but an opportunity to consider Indianness, Europeanness, and mestizo-ness as perspective bound, politically weighted mental constructs. Aztlán and the borderlands are therefore not the impossibilities they are for the nation states of the United States and Mexico but the open possibility for negotiating difference.

Three years after writing "El Plan Espiritual de Aztlán," Alurista revised his words for the introduction to his volume of poetry, *Nationchild Plumaroja*. This revision was more gender sensitive and more Indian. What had been in the plan "Brotherhood unites us, and love for our brothers . . ." becomes in the poetry, "brotherhood and sisterhood unites us, and love for our brothers and sisters. . . ." The language became less gender specific, but Chicanos became more Indian. Instead of being mestizos, "a bronze people with a bronze culture," Chicanos became "a Red People with a Red Culture." And because Red Chicanos "do not recognize capricious borders on the Red Continent," that is, because they are fully indigenous, there was no reason to locate Aztlán according to any nation-state perspective: "the northern land of Aztlán" became "our motherland Aztlán."

Nevertheless, Alurista's redefinition is plausible because, given the parameters of the hybrid subject, multiple, and even contradictory, positions are possible. In other words, within caló and within the cultural nationalist epic, it is possible to conceive the self, to conceive the Chicano subject, in any combination of the defining forces. The Chicano is at once mestizo and Indian, and the mestizo or Indian lives in the United States and/or Aztlán and speaks English and/or Spanish.[20] And beyond this, the subject is hybridized, meaning that there is always the possibility of the subject's active participation in that definition.

If one can imagine that for the Chicano subject language figures in as the language of languages, one can also imagine how hybrid subjectivity is played out in a difrasismo of difrasismos. This broad cultural difrasismo seems to me to characterize the Chicano subject. Not only does it yoke together different elements, it keeps present the separate elements and the new concept it creates. It is not quite dialectic or metaphor, nor does it efface the originals in the new. It is a sign of hybridizing, of leaving bare the work of coming to be. And for Chicanos the real presence of the Indian in the mestizo body is not mere metaphor, nor is the international borderline, but the real elements of our bodies, our homes, our languages that set us to the task of being. And yet Aztlán is a myth, the borderlands an argument, and poetry illogical.

I conclude with a personal note. I was in New York the year after

Alurista published *Nationchild Plumaroja,* and I arranged for him to come out and do his first readings so far outside Aztlán.[21] His reading at Columbia was attended by the handful of Chicano students there and by some other Chicanos doing other work in New York, including Dolores Huerta. In speaking with Alurista, I mentioned that I was about to become a father but confessed that we had no name for the baby. He shamed me, saying that as a poet I had no excuse for not coming up with a fine name. He was right. When my daughter was born, I named her Marisol, Sea and Sun in Spanish, a name I mistakenly thought I had invented. I gave her a name that is a difrasismo, and she is the one who chooses what combination of Sea and/or Sun she configures herself to be. I named her two sisters in bilingual difrasismos, Xóchitl Dolores (Nahuatl and Spanish) and Mireya Alba (Provençal and Spanish). And likewise, they can articulate themselves as they see fit.

Sex and Color

Respuesta a Frida

11/2, X4

On n'est pas morte mais déjà presque vivante, presque née,
en train de naître peut-être, dans ce passage hors frontière et
hors temps qui caractérise le désir. Désir de l'autre, désir du
monde. . . . Traverser l'opacité du silence et inventer nos
existences, nos amours, là où il n'y a plus de fatalité d'aucune
sorte.

– Marie Uguay

Q. F. –

[*cctbc,* Frida,
y *ccsa* letra *tdg* a
kiss, a lacuna. Each
drop of letter, yes, is
a fall of sorts.
Socc. So cae cada
gota, some heaven
missed.

2 color: Frieda 2 Frida,
I write *2u* Frida las 2, *at,*
cuata *d2* misma cuata,
cuerpo *d2* mismo cuerpo,
F-Kerida, ambas
Frida, la misma *d2*

misma, Frieda.
at, 1 última respuesta:
en la cuna de las letras vacías,
echo el son hueco de un huerco,
y tras la arena de tierra y tiempo,
se suelta tu eco.]

I am sorry such time has passed since you dropped me off
that last letter. It is fall still in California and so much
frigid earth between us (el otoño gris, Frida, California
fría). I close my eyes as I write now (te rías). I can see
your brown eyes, your brow, your row of black braids
(O yes you're you, yet your own image becomes mine in my
mind's eye, becomes our own in the blank of the letter o yes)
and black snakes curve above your head.

— AA

[Cuento
1 pierna, 1 ceja, 1 nacimiento,
2 Fridas, 3 ojos, unos picotazos, más sangre.
Menos 1 letra
(verde, el kalor alemán de Frieda la judía)
menos 1 letra
(trieste, la de una narrativa del único dolor posible
de andar quebrada en mala hora).
Encuentro
Frida menos la letra,
Frida, con una sola ceja, el plumado européo,
Frida la cuata tehuana, la cojita,
Frida menos la letra.]

P.S. —
"Se van como pájaros, de volada, like clumps of cut hair,
each strand and bird signifying great love." Como cartas a
los muertos and the soft clothing, buti suave, of the loved
one. And the sobres amarillos, llenos de cartas llenas de

letras de los desaparecidos, such yellow butterflies in the
air about me como las últimas letras de sexo, como *eso*.

[la cuna vacía, sin son, sin *bb,*
2 las *2,* parecidas, *2d* la letra
desaparecida, Frida, en fin,
d parte *d* mí, *atnlD.F., Q.F.,* desde
X4 today, this last letter, I write
"*Q.F.,*" florecida en caló. *2*flor yo canto,
color de caló:
trieste, colorado, y de aztlán.]

Y en fin, *F,*
¿quién más falta la letra?
¿la poeta que ahora canta en caló, o
el pintor que miró un color
encarnado por los límites de todos los
ayeres, o
la lectora que apretará en las manos,
al acabar de leer, una vida literalmente
vaciada?

Just as,
venadita,
the eighteen letters = las quince letras,
we come *bbn*
la cuna of the letter.

Heterotextual Reproduction

In the beginning, Octavio Paz defined the genesis of mexicanidad in the story of sexualized contact between Hernán Cortés and la Malinche, conquistador and translator, European and American, man and woman. The Mexican Nobel laureate's mid-twentieth-century retelling of the historical intercourse, by then four and a half centuries old, served to clarify and to sharpen a people's self-conception as a bastard race, as *hijos de la chingada*. But to be hijos de la chingada, Paz informs us, is so much more than being a bastard race, and to be Mexican is so much more than being half Old World European and half New World American. For the Mexican is a product of the miscegenation of Spanish *men* and Indian *women,* and to be so means to be the product of cataclysmic cultural intercourse. Whether in Mexico or Aztlán, the Mexican and Chicano subjects' nascence is narrated in the history and in the mythology of colonial and sexual encounter.[1]

For Octavio Paz, the Malinche/Cortés history and myth, let us call it "text," is most significant for its effects on Mexican psychology because it writes Mexicans as bastard descendents of a sexualized conquest, that is, as hijos de la chingada. In this sense, the meaning of the Malinche/Cortés text lies in its promulgation of a subjectivity that vacillates between the poles of the *chingón* and the *chingada*. Briefly and loosely, this can be translated into English as the poles of the *one-who-fucks-over* and the *one-who's-fucked-over*. This translation suffices because it retains the elements of both sex and aggression, even if *fuck* is etymologically more sexual than is *chingar*.[2] Paz's schema of Mexicans as of hijos de la chingada is a pronouncement by the nation's preeminent poet-philosopher that simultaneously explains and affirms the national myth: something important happened when two people had sex, and its effects are felt to this day.

The "what" of what happened is of course especially consequential: amid the other acts of conquest and colonization of Mexico, sexual intercourse produced a new race.[3] The facts of this are clear. In 1519 Cortés landed in Mexico with six hundred men, and in two years had conquered the Aztecs, whose metropolis, Tenochtitlan, was the most populous in the world. He was able to do so because he allied the diverse people he conquered, most notably the Tlaxcalans, in his campaign against the Aztecs. And he was able to do that, at least in part, because he had the services of a native translator, la Malinche.[4] In addition, Malinche and Cortés produced a half-breed son. The meaning of this begins simply: mestizo people have in Malinche and Cortés the mother and father of their hybrid race. This means that Mexicans and Chicanos are made up in body and in culture of the stuff of that union, and this meaning has very profound effects on subject formation.

What I am concerned with here is *that* meaning. Chicano subjectivity posits as central metaphor that it is mestizo and that its constitutive mode is hybridization. The body of that subject is racially hybrid, the product of the miscegenation of immigrant European and indigenous American peoples. The genesis of the mestizo occurs at the colonial encounter, coming to be first in the violent conquest.[5] After the conquest, the mestizo came to be reproduced as part of the larger colonial project. This means that today the act of being mestizo is an act of working out various cultural tendencies, piecing out a subjectivity within the parameters of hybridity. The sense of being mestizo-Chicano was born in the acts of colonial sex, yet is engendered daily in the conflicts of cultural elements, conflicts that are conceived as sexualized interactions.

So I am concerned with sex; I am concerned with texts. The mestizo body is made through sexual intercourse, specifically through the biologic interplay of different sexes, through heterosexual reproduction. The Chicano subject comes about through the interplay of different social "texts," analogously, through *heterotextual* reproduction. The physical body is born and reproduces, and analogously, the cultural subject has genesis and reproduction. Which brings me to the question: what of the analog of sexual reproduction for cultural reproduction?

The Chicano subject is a hybrid subject, beginning with the racial hybridity brought about by the disseminating of genes in the colonial project. Attendant with the half-breed, the mongrel, the crossblood, the mestizo body is the hybrid subject: chicanismo is the site of cultural confluence. The social texts of "race," of "language," and of "religion," for example, participate in the intercourse of a subject born of dialogue. The Chicano's subjectivity is heterotextual because diverse texts compete for presence and because their interaction is conceived according to an analog of intercourse that is sexualized and gendered. Mestizos came about, in almost every case, like that of Cortés and Malinche, because of sex between a Spanish man and an Indian woman. And because of this, the textual interaction is sexualized and gendered: Catholicism, the Spanish language, the Western system of writing, all descend to mestizos from the father. The conquest was particularized in sexual and gender relations so that the conquistador father could destroy the native culture and native body, and infuse his own. This began with the mass slaying of Indian men so that in defeating the native military, the conquistador greatly reduced the potentiality of native paternity.[6] Native progeny was eliminated, too, as in the practice of feeding Indian children to Spanish dogs.[7] Indian women were raped and made mothers of the conquistadors' offspring. The mestizo is the bastard offspring, the child of rape who speaks the father's language and attends the father's church.

So the intertextuality of chicanismo is modeled after the heterosexual intercursive relations of colonialism. But not only is the hybrid subjectivity founded at the heterotextual encounter, it is proliferated by a system of heterotextual reproduction. This is to say, the hybrid subject envisions an articulation of self that emerges from the continued acts of hybridization. Because the hybrid subject descends from at least two competing strains, a paradigm of monolineal descent, such as parthenogenetic reproduction within a single culture, is not appropriate. On the other hand, a paradigmatic ideal of monolineal, homocultural purity would be relatively more appropriate for nonhybridizing, monological peoples. This was relatively the case for the colonial Spaniard, who, despite profound cultural heterogeneity, could idealize himself as "pure" Spanish in relation to his half-breed mestizo children.[8] For Mexicans and for Chicanos subjectivity is reproduced anew in the self-fashioning act of heterotextual interaction. But this sense is more acute for the Chicano than for the Mexican because the Chicano derives *being* not only from the Spanish colonial intervention but also from Anglo-American colonialism: for not only was Mexico conquered by Spain, but Northern Mexico by the United States. It is this second colonization that so profoundly informs the contemporary Chicano reconsideration of a self formed from conflict.

Thus it is recently that Chicanos have come to terms with the subject. The subject of hybridity plays itself out in heterotextual discourse, conceived from the model of heterosexual intercourse, according to which, Chicano subjectivity is understood to reproduce. The synchronic implication of cultural genesis and the diachronic implication of cultural transmission are considered in light of the double colonization, the Spanish of Mexico and the U.S. American of Aztlán, the territory that formerly comprised northern Mexico, from Texas to California.[9]

Contemporary Chicano investigation of the subject has led to its greater complexity, if for no other reason than a reading of hybridity that introduces new texts compounds the factors of heterotextuality. This reconsideration of the Chicano not only incorporates the American colonial experience but takes aim at major tenets of Mexican mestizaje. These investigations focus on several poles of textual activity: on the texts of "father," on the matter of heterosexuality as paradigm, and on the possibility of alternate models for conceiving cultural reproduction. Three writers have focused their attention here: Rolando J. Romero, Gloria Anzaldúa, and Cherríe Moraga. The three have problematized matters of gender, patriarchy, and sexual orientation within the colonial context. Their work has entered into debate with notions of the hybrid subject that are linked to the specific detail and sense of the Malinche/Cortés paradigm of genesis and cultural transmission.

Romero's strategy in "Texts, Pre-Texts, Con-Texts: Gonzalo Guerrero in the Chronicles of Indies" is simple: he opposes the Malinche/Cortés "text" of mestizo genesis and reproduction with another "text." This dialogue of opposition is especially effective in two areas: the Gonzalo Guerrero text overturns the historical primacy of the Malinche/Cortés text, and it reconceives colonial patriarchy and the role of the father.

In the first instance, the story of Gonzalo Guerrero challenges the story of Malinche and Cortés, that is, it posits a narrative and history that recontextualizes the former narrative and history. The story of Gonzalo Guerrero does not oppose the actual history of Malinche and Cortés, it supplements, yet in doing so radically reshapes its meaning. It neither refutes their act of sexual intercourse nor denies their biologic reproduction and the production of mestizo offspring. What it does do is to overturn the semantic impact of Malinche and Cortés as the historical analogs of the mythical Adam and Eve. It does so very simply: it states that Malinche and Cortés were not, after all, first.

In the second instance, the Gonzalo Guerrero text undermines colonial patriarchy and affords a complete reconfiguration of the role of the father of the mestizo. The significance of Cortés as Adam is not only that he is the Ur-father of the race but also that he is the source of culture, for it was Adam who preceded Eve and who named the objects in the world. Analogously, Cortés and Adam brought about language, inseminating woman and disseminating sense. But unlike Adam, Cortés was not first; Gonzalo Guerrero preceded Cortés and acted in quite a different manner. In fact, the power relations of conqueror and conquered were so different that the Gonzalo text presents a narrative of a wholly other colonial patriarchy.

The traditional mythical story of Mexican genesis and the history of conquest intertwine in a narrative that climaxes in the intercourse of extremely different people, Spaniard and Indian, man and woman, and so on. After Columbus, Cortés proved the single most potent founding father of the Spanish Empire, which he did by defeating the largest New World empire. The vast differences between the worlds old and new and the tremendous economic value of the conquest make the work of Cortés and the role of Malinche extremely consequential. This is true. But Rolando Romero tells us that further encomium, the inscription of Cortés as founding father of a new race, is just not true.

Then, coupled with the mythicized conquistador, there is Malinche.

Her significance, even before that of being Eve and mother, is that of translator. Originally she was used so that Cortés could form alliances with the Indians he conquered, an effort for which he promised her, her freedom. She served as the communication bridge between Europe and America, negotiating, for example, between Cortés and Moctezuma. In all of this, her discursive activity operated at the center of the conquest. She also had sex with the conquistador. Cortés gave her over to one of his soldiers, but after the soldier returned to Spain, she lived with Cortés for a while in a house that still stands in Mexico City.[10] They did not marry, but they did have one son, Martín, whom Cortés named after his father. The relationship of the user and the one used is what is recalled in the relationship as chingón and chingada. In any case, her role did, as did that of Cortés, intertwine participation in the conquest with the begetting of a hybrid race.

Romero traces the uncelebrated but documented history of Gonzalo Guerrero, who unlike Cortés, left no words in his own hand.[11] Eight years before Cortés landed in Mexico, some seventeen Spaniards shipwrecked off Jamaica, eventually landing in Yucatán in 1511.[12] One was Gonzalo Guerrero. Like Cortés, but before, Guerrero produced mestizo offspring with an Indian woman. But his relation to the Indian woman, his role as father, and his participation in the colonial project were in so many ways different from those of Cortés. He may have been a Spanish man, but his role in some ways more approximated that of Malinche.

Malinche had been given to Cortés as a slave, part of a group of twenty women who were to become the first baptized Christians in New Spain. Gonzalo Guerrero was enslaved by the Mayans and became the first Spaniard to assimilate Mexican–Indian language, religion, culture. Malinche and Gonzalo both embraced the opposing culture and did so as slaves. When Cortés landed in Mexico, he tried but was unable to recruit Gonzalo to aid in the conquest as translator and guide: Gonzalo could not be reached. Cortés instead acquired the services of Jerónimo de Aguilar, Gonzalo's fellow castaway. Because Aguilar spoke Mayan, his translation skills were of limited value in the Aztec Empire until the multilingual, Nahuatl- and Mayan-speaking, Malinche arrived. At first Cortés spoke Castilian to Aguilar, who spoke Mayan to Malinche, who spoke Nahuatl to the Indians; but Malinche soon acquired Spanish so Aguilar became superfluous.[13]

Gonzalo reportedly refused to support the Spanish effort because he was married and loved his children. He had assimilated to the culture of his captors completely: his body was tattooed and pierced, he spoke their language, and he had not only produced offspring but married according to Mayan custom. The degree of his assimilation can be envisioned by considering that of Jerónimo de Aguilar. When the Spanish found Aguilar, they did not recognize him as a European; he was naked and spoke poor Spanish. He could not even eat European food: even his digestive system had gone native. Gonzalo Guerrero married his slave master, yet it is possible to construct a narrative, as it is for Malinche, that includes some degree of volition in the process of assimilation. After all, Cortés promised Malinche freedom if she aided his cause; perhaps the same is true of Gonzalo: one version of his life has him completely converted, eventually dying in combat against the Spaniards. In 1528, nine years after Cortés's unsuccessful contact with Gonzalo, Francisco de Montejo tried the same in his bid to conquer Yucatán. Supposedly Gonzalo refused, saying, in part, "Look how beautiful my children are."[14]

It is here that the Gonzalo Guerrero text makes such radical change. Here the father makes children in the image of the mother, and it is the father who embraces the other culture. This is not the model of paternity that bears the authority for the source of culture; it is not the father that transmits the law, language, religion, political power. Instead Gonzalo Guerrero provides an image of an effaced paternity, of the father who rejects the colonial project. This is a notion of the father that embraces alterity, and for this the Gonzalo Guerrero text is censured, ignored, condemned.[15] Gonzalo's narrative is either denigrated or dropped from history.

The relative success of colonialism is predicated on masculine authority animated in the precept of the phallus. The history-myth of Cortés is particularly rigid, combining as it does the lustre of the Adam and Eve myth, an incredibly potent militarism, and an original begetting. It combines the weight of myth and history, violence and sex. The Gonzalo text provides an alternative narrative, one that renders suspect the absolute authority of Cortés and the patriarchal, colonial project. Gonzalo loved his *Indian* children; he did not feed them to dogs. This alone opposes the history of genocide born with Cortés that would eliminate 95 percent of the native population in the first century of colonialism. It also demonstrates that culture need not necessarily flow solely from the patriarchal source, that is, Gonzalo's history demonstrates that while the father can inseminate, he can be culturally inseminated as well.

For Cortés, it was vital to be the first and sole colonial patriarch, and ironically, he sought to base his claim as such in the fact of Gonzalo Guerrero's prior presence. In the politics of empire, Cortés had to negotiate his own claim to the newly discovered territory of Mexico amid the competing imperial claims of king and governor. Romero argues that Guerrero and Aguilar's presence in Yucatán enabled Cortés to argue that the governor in Cuba had no right to Mexico and "Whoever brought Guerrero and Aguilar into their camp could thus claim to have a right to the territory, or at the very least, prove that Diego Velázquez had not inherent right to the new lands" (348). In this way, Gonzalo Guerrero presented no threat to Cortés and served as no competing patriarch. Even Gonzalo's children, being Indians, posed no competition to Cortés's progeny.

In developing the project he calls "Gonzalo Guerrero as Counter Malinche," Rolando Romero radically rewrites the patriarchy that serves as basic structure for the notions of genesis and reproduction of the Chicano subject. "Father" is no longer the colonial agent, but becomes instead a relatively passive contributor to the gene pool. It is a radical revision, yet, nevertheless, two things remain similar: one, "father" remains the site of one-way cultural transmission, either, on the one hand, inseminating or, on the other, assimilating; and two, heterosexual reproduction remains the central analog. Gonzalo Guerrero alters the colonial paradigm to be sure, but it remains centered on the father and his sexual activity.

The Chicano subject is affected profoundly by all of this, particularly so in the areas of gender and power relations. According to Octavio Paz, the politics of the sexual encounter mark Cortés and Malinche as chingón and chingada. This aligns the markers "man,"

"European," and "father" with colonial authority, power, and machismo. "Woman," "Indian," and "mother" align with a passive femininity, except where actively supporting the conquistador against the native population. Paz allows that a man may be passive, may be chingado in the affairs of men; the Aztec warrior, for example, was chingado by Cortés. Romero's articulation of the Gonzalo text opens up a new range of possibilities: Gonzalo's wife was his master, effectively she was chingona and he chingado.[16] Bernal Díaz del Castillo notes authority in her words to Aguilar when he tried to recruit Gonzalo, "And Gonzalo's Indian wife spoke to Aguilar very angrily in her own language: 'Why has this slave come here to call my husband away? Go off with you, and let us have no more of your talk' " (61). Bernal Díaz del Castillo also notes that Malinche refuses to be chingona, acquiescing completely to the Spanish patriarchs,

> saying that God had been very gracious to her in freeing her from the worship of idols and making her a Christian, and giving her a son by her lord and master Cortes, also in marrying her to such a gentleman as her husband Juan Jaramillo. Even if they were to make her mistress of all the provinces of New Spain, she said, she would refuse the honour, for she would rather serve her husband and Cortes than anything else in the world. What I have related here I know for certain and swear to. (86)

In the Gonzalo Guerrero text, very simply, the masculine is allowed passivity before the feminine, this demonstrated by the passive assimilation of the most masculine of exemplars, the Spanish conquistador, before an Indian woman. In a more complex way, sexuality, passivity, and responsibility are rewritten as well. For Paz, that Malinche is chingada means that a sexually passive role combines with compliance with the colonial project so that she is used up by the Spanish Empire and then discarded. Furthermore, she is spurned for having slept willingly with the enemy and having been instrumental in the conquest and ensuing genocide, even though she acted as a slave. Her compliance while a slave parallels that of Gonzalo Guerrero.[17] For if we allow that Malinche's complicity in sex and politics is tempered by her position as a slave, the same can be allowed for Gonzalo. In this manner, Romero's reading of "man" and "father" is quite different from that of Paz, for in it lies the possibility of a patriarchy without authority. For in the power relations in slavery, is any slave, female or male, ever allotted full subjectivity? Isn't any sex between master and slave tacit rape?

And yet, even if sexual relations do figure prominently in the paradigms of cultural formation and transmission, they need not necessarily be heterosexual relations. Lesbian writers Gloria Anzaldúa and Cherríe Moraga approach the matter of Chicano subjectivity by emphasizing Anglo-American colonialism and by positing a paradigm of cultural reproduction with an analog of homosexual intercourse. In their discussion, the locale is the borderlands, the territory the United States conquered from Mexico, and the intercourse is woman to woman; and yet many of their concerns resonate with those of Romero. This is so because all three focus on key matters of subjectification: genesis and reproduction.

The title of Gloria Anzaldúa's work is telling, *Borderlands/La Frontera: The New Mestiza.* The site of new hybridizing is the border zone, the northern half of Mexico taken by the United States, the homeland Chicanos call Aztlán. For Anzaldúa, the material site of intercultural conflict supersedes the initial act of intercourse as the primary fact and condition of the hybrid subject. The border is a political marker that demarcates the reach of Anglo-American colonialism. It was created in violence, and to this day Mexicans north of that line, Chicanos, are subject to violent cultural wars. To be Chicano in California or Texas, for example, is to wage a dynamic subjectivity that pieces a self from the conflicting texts of Anglo-American, Mexican, Chicano.

Anzaldúa's locus of, and paradigm for, mestizaje is the borderlands, and in her vision, this zone for subject contention is highly sexualized. "The prohibited and forbidden are its inhabitants," she says, including "the perverse, the queer . . . , the mongrel . . . , the half-breed, the half dead" (3). The hybrid inhabitants are viewed by the powerful, "legitimate" whites as transgressors, transgressors not only of national boundaries but of sexual mores, including prescribed heterosexuality.[18] For Anzaldúa, sexuality, specifically sexual orientation, is a dynamic factor at play in the politics of the subject.

Borderlands/La Frontera begins with a violent image, "The U.S.-Mexican border *es una herida abierta* [an open wound] where the Third World grates against the first and bleeds. And before a scab forms it hemorrhages again, the lifeblood of two worlds merging to form a third country – a border culture" (3). The image of the genesis of the hybrid subject is in violence to the body, in a wound, and its reproduction transpires in a rupture, in the continual reopening of that wound. The paradigm of heterosexual reproduction is supplanted by that of international violence. According to this paradigm, the transmitting medium of culture is not semen but blood.

Bloodshed engenders a "third country – a border culture." The violence of Anglo-American colonialism, both in the establishment and in the maintenance of rule over the borderlands, is, ironically, a generative force. For what comes about there amid the struggles between economic worlds, between nations, between cultures is a hybrid alternative. This alternative is not so much racial, as in the synthesis of the mestizo, as it is cultural. There they speak a "bastard language, Chicano Spanish, [that] is not approved by any society": an alternative language for the making of alternative space, the third country *between* the United States and Mexico.

Borderlands/La Frontera is less concerned with reproducing the body than it is with producing new consciousness. Because of this, the procreative role of the father is bypassed, as is the more general patriarchal imperative. There is no need for the primacy of heterosexual reproduction since the object for reproduction is the cultural subject and not the body. What Anzaldúa sees as the potential product of the borderlands is "la conciencia de la mestiza," a new mestiza consciousness. It displaces traditional patriarchy because it is gynocentric, and further, it is not particularly rooted in sexual reproduction.

The hybridity that pervades the new mestiza subject manifests a concomitant ambiguity. Heterogeneous forces impinge upon borderlands subjects and create ambiguities in the social and in the personal spheres. Anzaldúa cites the new mestiza's tolerance for ambiguity as the very means to oppose the closed texts of Western binarism that prescribe heterosexuality, patriarchal authority, and intolerance for deviation. In explaining how the ambiguous third country – border culture – is manifested in the personal subject, Anzaldúa posits homosexuality as an alternative to prescribed heterosexuality and to either/ or gender differentiation. She states, "I like other queer people, am two in one body, both male and female. I am the embodiment of the *hieros gamos:* the coming together of opposite qualities within" (19). In this manner, Anzaldúa describes an alternative third gender, one that is oriented not toward reproduction of the body but toward the reproduction of culture. The lesbian mestiza pits tolerance for ambiguity and alternate gender identification against the rigid heterosexual prescription. This position is active, she chooses to be this way, choosing, even, to be lesbian; as she says, "I made the choice to be queer" (19).

Since the new consciousness is elected by choice and since the object of production is consciousness rather than the body, the mestiza's subjectivity can be widely inclusive. It is not inherited from sexual intercourse like race but is taken on in response to the ambient forces of repression. When she considers the scope of that repression, Anzaldúa embraces nearly everyone as potential subject of the new consciousness, for nearly everyone is marginalized in some way in the borderlands. Not quite everyone is included, however; she rejects the purest incarnation of patriarchy, the white male heterosexual. It is perhaps at this point that she is most adamant in her opposition to patriarchal politics, for clearly the white male heterosexual has the most invested in the texts "father," "colonialism," and "phallus."

The problem of the father is taken up further in Cherríe Moraga's *The Last Generation*. Moraga undertakes a project very similar to Anzaldúa's in that she also explores hybridity as a lesbian Chicana response to Anglo-American domination. The similarity of their focus and strategy is evidenced in their 1981 collaboration *This Bridge Called My Back: Writings by Radical Women of Color*, which they coedited. Both writers deploy the texts "woman" and "lesbian" to heterotextually undermine the homotextual monologue articulated by patriarchy and compulsory heterosexuality.

Borderlands/La Frontera and *Last Generation* both work out textually what they advocate in content, that is, they are literary hybrids that propose a hybrid subjectivity. They are truly heterotexts, admixtures of genres and of languages. Each work combines essay, testimony, and poetry in a dialogue that actively resists simple definition. And the dialogue is carried on interlingually as well: both texts mix English, Spanish, Chicano slang, and some Nahuatl in a verbal interplay that replicates the interplay of speech acts in the borderlands. This linguistic hybridity is especially telling, because for both Anzaldúa and Moraga it is an index of both the resistance to colonialism and the propagation of cultural alternatives. In this way, interlingualism forms the basis for intercultural relations in the lesbian model similar to the way heterosexuality does in the patriarchal.[19]

Interlingual hybridized speech is so integral a mode of articulation in the borderlands that Chicano subjectivity itself comes to be born and reproduced in the act. "I am my language," says Anzaldúa. For her to be so, mestiza articulation must oppose silent acquiescence to what she calls the "cultural tyrannies" of white colonial rule and its obdurate patriarchy. The mestiza subject must manifest and transmit culturally, that is, she must articulate homosexual texts heterotextually, dialogically. The genesis and reproduction of the mestiza must arise in the active and perlocutionary speech act.[20] In this way, reproduction is imagined to occur in an act of the tongue, the lesbian, female tongue, and not in the act of the phallus.

Yet while the tongue can displace the phallus and engender consciousness, it cannot produce bodies. And too, the product of this reproduction, the cultural hybrid subject, is more tenuous than the physical mestizo body, relying as it does on choice and performance in language. It is with this in mind that Cherríe Moraga reexamines heterosexual reproduction and the place of the body in culture. *The Last Generation* is, as she says, "a prayer at a time when I no longer remember how to pray"; it is a hopeful invocation, yet an apocalyptic vision.

Last Generation is an act of writing the subject in a historical moment of crisis, beyond which perhaps lies annihilation. Moraga worries that she may be the end of the line, that her words may be the last lines. Her analog for the present crisis is the catastrophic end of the

Aztec world with the fact of the Spanish conquest. In this way she conflates cultural annihilation with genocide, the end of the subject with the end of the body.

> In 1524, just three years after the Spanish Conquest of the Aztec Empire, the Náhuatl sages, the tlamatinime, came before the missionary friars in defense of their religion. "Our gods are already dead," they stated. "Let us perish now." Their codices lay smoldering in heaps of ash.
>
> I write with the same knowledge, the same sadness, recognizing the full impact of the colonial "experiment" on the lives of Chicanos, mestizos, and Native Americans. Our codices – dead leaves unwritten – lie smoldering in the ashes of disregard, censure, and erasure. *The Last Generation* emerges from those ashes. I write it against time, out of a sense of urgency that Chicanos are a disappearing tribe, out of a sense of this disappearance in my own familia. (2)

She may be the last generation, her culture and her body may fail to reproduce. To combat this, she writes; she articulates textually and fixes a potent identity: "I call myself a Chicana writer. Not a Mexican–American writer, not an Hispanic writer, not a half-breed writer. To be a Chicana is not merely to name one's racial/cultural identity, but also to name a politic, a politic that refuses assimilation into the U.S. mainstream" (56). Being Chicana is a politics of refusal to disappear, but it is not, in and of itself, a politics of reproduction.

Moraga's concerns for reproducing the body of culture coincide with, and perhaps emerge from, her concerns for reproducing her own body. She locates the generational crisis in a personal one: she turns forty, has borne no children, and exists in a culture that dictates that she reproduce. Moraga's concern for her body is at once her concern with how the social inscription impinges upon the physical and with how the physical reproduces the social. The personal so readily melds with the social in the nexus of physical reproduction. This is the topos of the title essay in *Last Generation;* Moraga's concerns focus on the conjunction of the personal and the social in the reproductive arena of the family:

At my fortieth birthday party, my tíos and tías sit talking around the dinner table. Most are in their late seventies now, and I notice their whitening hair and frail bodies, their untiring dignity. I relish the sound of their elegant and common Spanish, the subtlety of their humor and vividness of their recovered memories, their cuentos. Watching them, I know lo mexicano will die with their passing. My tío's children have not taught their own children to be Mexicans. They have become "Americans." And we're all supposed to quietly accept this passing, this slow and painless death of a cultura, this invisible disappearance of a people. But I do not accept it, I write. I write as I always have, but now I write for a much larger family. (2)

My family is beginning to feel its disintegration. Our Mexican grandmother of ninety-six years has been dead two years now and la familia's beginning to go. Ignoring this, it increases in number. I am the only one who doesn't ignore this because I am the only one not contributing to the population. My line of family stops with me. There will be no one calling me, *Mami, Mamá, Abuelita.* . . .

I am the last generation put on this planet to remember and record. (9)

In the course of this narrative, she recounts again and again how she is disappearing into the sofa. At the family gathering, where the bodies are fertile but the subjects sterile, she is the last generation. She is disappearing into the sofa: sinking out of sight; and disappearing into the sofa: turning into furniture, a fixture, an object. While her family reproduces the body at the expense of the subject, she writes to remember and record. Yet she disappears. She links the matter of reproducing the body with that of reproducing the subject so that personally she loses subjectivity, she reifies, sinking into an object. Clearly she evokes the heterosexual paradigm, but to what end?

In the ensuing story "The Ecology of Woman," Moraga narrates a heterosexual encounter in Mexico. The intercourse may be heterosexual, but the subject remains lesbian. Cecilia remains distant from men, taking charge in sex with a boy, for example, and avoiding the Mexican soldiers, men and their real guns. She bathes away the scent of the boy and dreams of women and that she is pregnant. She dreams of a daughter who can confirm her subjectivity, a daughter who will confer maternity and "who will call her mami and forgive her the calling of her own mother's name for the last time." But menstruation disrupts the dream, "For three days, she gives birth / to her own motherless / blood" (23).

Recall that for Anzaldúa, the new mestiza is born in the open wound of cultural conflict and that bloodshed engenders the new subjectivity. But for Moraga, blood flow is sterile. Both Anzaldúa and Moraga imagine paradigmatic shifts in consciousness brought on by linguistic articulation, and both do so as an alternative to compulsory heterosexuality. Both offer lesbian subjectivity in the face of an oppressive patriarchy: they undermine the text "father." But what of "mother"? For Moraga, heterosexuality remains problematic, but she nevertheless tries to recuperate "mother." Clearly she does not embrace colonial patriarchy, but in her concern to reproduce the body, she once again takes up the problem of heterosexual intercourse. For Moraga it is a problem that is not easily dismissed, if only for its reproductive capability.

Moraga's recuperation of "mother" recalls Romero's recuperation of "father." By employing the heterotextual interplay of the Gonzalo Guerrero narrative as counter-Malinche narrative, Romero rewrites the facts of colonial patriarchy. Moraga rewrites the colonized "mother" after the facts of the U.S. and Spanish colonial patriarchies and after the theorization of a borderlands mestiza subjectivity. In very different ways, Moraga and Romero retain a central significance for heterosexual reproduction: she, by supplementing homosocial desire with the desire to reproduce the body; and he, by radically refashioning paternity in many ways except for its primary, biological role.

Romero's work also supplements that of Anzaldúa in two areas, the suppression of the father and the general strategy of the heterotext. When Anzaldúa propounds the new mestiza consciousness, she constructs a hybrid, borderlands subject that comes to be in reaction to colonial patriarchy. Part of the new consciousness is possession of "la facultad," "the capacity to see in surface phenomena the meaning of deeper realities." For Anzaldúa, the borderlands subject is the marginalized who develop la facultad in response to oppression, "[T]hose who are pounced on the most have it the strongest – the females, the homosexuals of all races, the darkskinned, the outcast, the persecuted, the marginalized, the foreign" (38).

At the site of concentrated colonial repression, the white father is excluded because he determines marginalization, because he does the marginalizing. In "Border of Fear, Border of Desire," Romero observes the extreme opposition to the white father in the Plan de San Diego, a 1915 manifesto that called for the armed retaking of lands north of the Rio Grande.[21] Similar to Anzaldúa's union of the oppressed, the Plan called for a union of the Latin, Negro, and Japanese races against Anglo-American domination. But in a more extreme rejection of the white father, the Plan called for the death of every North American male over sixteen. This goes far beyond a call for unity among the oppressed; it is a call to terminate the traditional and extant patriarchy. In this way, the Plan turns the acts of the colonial project against itself by subjecting it to the erasure of the father. But then, in a move similar to his work on Gonzalo Guerrero, Romero offers another image of paternity, citing in the same article the work of José Vasconcelos. Vasconcelos is philosopher of the Mexican nationalism that glorified the mestizo as the raza cósmica, the union of racial extremes of humanity. Vasconcelos profoundly shapes Anzaldúa's new mestiza consciousness, and perhaps most significantly, as Romero points out, Vasconcelos is a borderlands Mexican whose quotidian life crossed the Rio Grande. It is as if, in relation to the violence of the Plan de San Diego, Romero offers a more passive, but culturally significant, patriarch.

It is in this way that Romero's use of the heterotext supplements the endeavors of Anzaldúa. Romero introduces José Vasconcelos and Gonzalo Guerrero as alternate texts, philosophy on the one hand, history on the other. Each provides a powerful means for conceiving racial mestizaje and cultural hybridity. Anzaldúa undertakes a similar effort by turning to the texts of myth and religion. She supplements the negative rejection of colonial patriarchy with the positive use of the heterotext. The alternate vision Anzaldúa provides is precisely that, a vision; with a firm basis in Aztec religion, she describes "the *Coatlicue* state." The recourse to the Aztec goddess Coatlicue provides the mestiza subject the heterotextuality of alternate religious experience. Anzaldúa describes a lesbian, Aztec-influenced rapture that infuses the new subjectivity; she describes the Coatlicue state:

> Shock pulls my breath out of me. The sphincter muscle tugs itself up, up, and the heart in my cunt starts to beat. A light is all around me – so intense it could be white or black or at that juncture where extremes turn into their opposites. It passes through my body and comes out of the other side. I collapse into myself – a delicious caving into myself – imploding, the walls like matchsticks softly folding inward in slow motion.
>
> I see *oposición e insurrección*. I see the crack growing on the rock. I see the fine frenzy building. I see the heat of anger or rebellion or hope split open that rock, releasing *la Coatlicue*. And someone in me takes matters into our own hands, and eventually, takes dominion over serpents – over my own body, my sexual activity, my soul, my mind my weaknesses and strengths. Mine. Ours. Not the heterosexual white man's or the colored man's or the state's or the culture's or the religion's or the parents' – just ours mine.
>
> And suddenly I feel everything rushing to a center, a nucleus. All the lost pieces of myself come flying from the deserts and the mountains and the valleys, magnetized toward that center. *Completa*.
>
> Something pulsates in my body, a luminous thin thing that grows thicker every day. Its presence never leaves me. I am never alone. That which abides: my vigilance, my thousand sleepless serpent eyes blinking in the night, forever open. And I am not afraid. (51)

Anzaldúa reworks Aztec mythology and provides an alternate, lesbian, Chicana experience. The rapture engenders something between the maternal goddess and the mestiza subject; something is produced and within the body, something grows every day. In a very basic way, the heterotextuality here is very like Romero's, the infusion of different texts has effect and produces something. And in a more specific way, Anzaldúa, like Moraga, confronts the issue of homosexual reproduction, but unlike Moraga, there is no turn to the heterosexual. Instead, the genesis and reproduction of cultural relations remains apart from the biologic; Anzaldúa describes a maternity without a requisite paternity.

All three writers, Rolando Romero, Gloria Anzaldúa, and Cherríe Moraga, have opened up dialogues with the colonial prescripts of "father" and "reproduction." Each one takes the mestizo hybrid subject to be the site of cultural conflict, and each compounds that conflict. They exploit a heterotextuality that supports the forces of hybridity and opposes those of monologic subjectivity. Their heterotexts oppose the paradigm of a cultural genesis and reproduction that is patriarchal, patronymic, and patrilineal. It is an attack equally on the father as analog of god and as Adam-the-namer and disseminator of language.

As a final note, it is worthwhile to consider that Adamic task of naming and ascribing language to things. In their own ways, Romero, Anzaldúa, and Moraga rename things; they employ their writing to refashion relationships in language in order to refashion relationships in consciousness and in the world. They write; they rename. After their texts "father" is not the same; "mestiza" is not the same.

Their work addresses the point that while we may know the name of the father, as in the case of Hernán Cortés, we are not given the real names of Malinche or of Gonzalo. This is so because the power to name and the right to bear name are meted out according to rules of the hegemony. We know Malinche, by the Nahuatl mispronunciation of Marina, her Christian name. And we do not know the names of the other women baptized with her, as Bernal Díaz observes: "I do not clearly remember the names of all the other women, and there is not reason for naming any of them. But they were the first women in New Spain to become Christians" (82). We do not know the surname of Gonzalo. We assume it is Guerrero, but it is just one of four attributed to him. We never know the name of his wife. Nor do we know the names of his children. They all remain ambiguous, poorly defined in comparison to the traditional father and his son: Hernán Cortés and Martín Cortés. It is clear that there is a politics in naming and being named.

Cherríe Moraga names herself, "I am a Chicana writer." Anzaldúa declares "I am my language." And Romero notes that while Malinche "was being called 'Doña Marina' by the Spaniards, Cortés was being addressed as 'Señor Malinche' by the indigenous people" (363). All three manipulate texts in an act of definition, in an act of articulating the self amid the forces of erasure. Romero locates the authority to name in the oppressed as well as in the oppressor. Anzaldúa locates her subjectivity in language itself. Moraga names herself as the subject agent, Chicana writer. She rejects silent acquiescence and nameless identity. She articulates, therefore she is; she speaks differently, therefore things are different.

Tricks of Gender Xing

When Europeans crossed the Atlantic "discovering" the New World, their boats may have lacked female sailors, but undoubtedly their minds were filled with that other and weaker sex. In the place of real women, they carried with them images and words, texts that could call to mind the absent body. Yet as they did, they kept her apart in the very act of bringing her along. For those texts defined woman in accordance with a principle of difference, which, regardless of how proximate the female body may be, always constructs it in absentia from the male. This ideological differentiation crossed the sea with those sailors and engendered the "discovery" of the "New World": it served as the conceptual grid upon which they wrote the spatial difference of the newly encountered place and the racial difference of the newly encountered people.[1] Consider two examples that illustrate the Spanish and English writing of the "New World." Some 460 years ago, Hernán Cortés found a new land and named it after a fictive island in *Las Sergas de Esplandián,* book five of *Amadís de Gaula.* Cortés saw in "California" what he had read in the chivalric romance: an island of riches and dark-skinned warrior women.[2] And perhaps the most telling expression of the English writing of America is John Donne's "To His Mistres Going to Bed":

> License my roaving hands, and let them go,
> Before, behind, between, above, below.
> O my America! my new-found-land,
> My kingdome, safeliest when with one man man'd,
> My Myne of precious stones, My Emperie,
> How blest am I in this discovering thee!

For Donne, "Woman" and "America" collapse into one discoverable and nameable other.

At the centers of the representational practices conceiving "New World," "America," and "Native," there operated some of the most fundamental precepts of Western patriarchal ideology.[3] And it is the nexus of "woman" and "writing," that is, "writing woman" and "woman writing," during the invention and conception of colonial America that concerns me here. I begin with the premise that European representations of American others were prefigured by European conceptions of gender. European conquest and colonization of Native America was conceived historically after the fact of the European male's subordination of the European female. I wish to focus on the time and place of colonial New Spain, to focus on the implications of the phenomenon of the New World woman writer. These implications demonstrate how Europe's reach across genders prefigured its reach across oceans, races, and epochs as well. In the case of Sor Juana, the New World woman writer crosses the straight and narrow line of masculist gender differentiation and then that of European race differentiation.

New World differences strained the old vocabularies and libraries; truly there were people, places, and things for which they had no names. The European could contain the newness of America as Cortés had, through the practices of representation, by encapsulating within the writing of the new the meanings contained in the old. Beginning with Columbus's emulation of Marco Polo, the discoverers read the Old World as they perceived and wrote a New. California, the Amazon, Nueva España, and New England all denoted new places yet connoted old texts. A name like "Nueva España" troped a relationship between old and new. The new was textualized as a spatial dislocation of the preexistent, the old stories and old civilizations in a new place. These Old World tropes textualized relationships across space and across time.

Old Muse, New Muse

In 1689 in Madrid, the capital of the Spanish Empire, there appeared an American text entitled *Inundación Castálida de la única poetisa, musa dézima, Soror Juana Inés de la Cruz;* it was a collection of writing by a New World woman writer. Text and author were described, as were other new phenomena, according to an old, familiar semantics. Sor Juana's writing was called *Inundación Castálida,* "Castalian Inundation," figuratively, poetic spill from the fountain of the muses. And she herself was named *musa décima,* the "tenth muse." And just as "California" refers to the new object in the terms and world view of the old subject, the term "tenth muse" encapsulates both neologism and archaism; the phenomenon of the New World woman writer is written according to an old European world view. The designation *musa décima,* of course, carries with it great symbolic value, but, in one sense, it functions literally as well, for Sor Juana wrote many ten-line *décimas.* So while she might have been the tenth muse figuratively, she was a décima poet literally. But the very allusion to the Greek muses writes Sor Juana in particular relation to the dominant cultural ideals. That is, from the vantage point of baroque, imperial Spain, the classicism of Greece and Rome could touch Spanish letters, and Spain itself, because of its tenth muse. By placing Sor Juana at the end of the line of the nine previous muses, *Calliope, Clio, Erato, Euterpe, Melpomene, Polyhymnia, Terpsichore, Thalia,* and *Urania,* the Spanish Siglo de oro could appear as living Terminus of the line from the classical Golden Age. The New World woman writer provided one means for the enhancement of the Spanish self.

Sor Juana's evocation as the tenth muse was not the first such troping of the New World woman writer. In 1650, in London, there was published Anne Bradstreet's *The Tenth Muse lately sprung up in America. or Severall Poems.* Generally, the conjunction of woman and writer in the New World was written similarly in England as it was in Spain.[4] The new phenomenon served as a means to validate the authority of a single line from the past: both Sor Juana and Anne Bradstreet were evoked as New World muses through whom the classical world could cross over to imperial Europe. Woman and America were evoked, then suppressed, as feminine others so that a metonymic link could be articulated with the classical male subject. In a very simple way, "tenth muse" asserts the contiguity of classical antiquity and imperial Europe, a continuity of cultural transmission from man to man. In such an exchange of authority, the presence of New World woman writer is fleeting: the tropic operation effaces both Americanness and femininity. The "tenth muse" is an imperial European celebration of Greek *poiesis,* after all, and neither the celebration of *in xóchitl in cuicatl,* Mexican poetics, nor that of feminist poetics.[5] But Sor Juana's poetics involves an even more complex tropics, one that gives woman a greater presence in the writing of America. Her texts cross the straight and narrow metonymic *line* of Eurocentric, masculist tropics with chiasmus.[6]

Sor Juana's Cross

After declaring its author the tenth muse, the title page of the *Inundación Castálida* describes its text as *varios metros, idiomas, y estilos,* "various meters, languages and styles." The description is accurate. Its diverse meters and styles range from short décimas and sonnets, to long villancicos and dramatic loas, to prose allegory – to cite a few examples. And there is diversity of yet another sort: the book is written in various languages. Good examples of this are the villancicos written in a dialog of voices in Spanish and Latin and a variety of other languages. "San Pedro Nolasco" and "Asunción" are two that include as part of their extensive heteroglossia a Nahuatl tocotín and Afro-Spanish dialect verse. In fact, these villancicos are among the very earliest representations of Afro-Spanish speech.[7] There is even tremendous discursive range within a single language, in the crossing of different social voices. Sor Juana's redondilla, "Hombres necios," is a protofeminist polemic that attacks masculist discourse for representing woman as the embodiment of masculine vice. This sort of discursive gender crossing was to achieve its fullest development in her intellectual autobiography, *La Repuesta a la Muy Ilustre Sor Filotéa de la Cruz,* published in 1691, one year after the "tenth muse" text. In "Hombres necios" and the *Respuesta,* Sor Juana directly confronts the misogynist heart of Eurocentric culture. The crossing of gendered discourses, as well as racial discourses, and the keen appropriation of Euro-male, homosocial rhetoric marks the "various meters, languages and styles" of Sor Juana, the New World woman poet.

Sor Juana's poetics stands in marked contrast to the simple metonymic linking practice of the "tenth muse" trope. When Anne Bradstreet undertakes the "Dialogue between Old England and New," for example, gender is presented in a relatively traditional way, race is ignored, and New World individuation is suppressed: Mother Old England dictates opposition to the Church of Rome, and Daughter New England embraces the colonial, and ultimately, patriarchal, single line of authority. But in "San Pedro Nolasco" and the *Respuesta,* Sor Juana undertakes a crossover poetics, intersecting competing lines of authority. And this textual activity is informed by Sor Juana's understanding of gender relations: she perceives New World racial alterity from her perspective of gender alterity. Cortés, Donne, and Bradstreet base their visions of America on a monolineal and traditional system of gender differentiation; Sor Juana is alone in basing hers on a bilineal and protofeminist one.[8]

I have chosen to characterize Sor Juana's poetics by the trope chiasmus and to call her rhetorical strategy chiastic tricks.[9] Chiasmus is a crossing of verbal elements. It is usually described as a figure of form, a grammatical crisscross in which the syntax in one line of verse is reversed in a second. The lines of corresponding elements, therefore, form a cross, an X. Chiasmus creates alternate syntax and each alternate line of opposed elements is invested with alternate meaning. It is in the propensity of crossed elements to provide crossed reading that chiasmus figures here. Chiasmus is related to metonymy, for its suppressive-adjunctive operation on syntax is similar to metonymy's on semantics.[10] Like metonymy, it orders meaning contiguously; but while metonymy is the trope of linearity and telos, chiasmus is the trope of the cross and opposition.

When the *Inundación Castálida* declares Sor Juana the latest in the sequence of classical muses, it asserts a metonymic relationship. "Tenth muse" is a combined neologism-archaism that affirms cultural continuity from Greece to Spain, at the expense of Sor Juana's femininity and Americanness. But if an alternate line were acknowledged, that of the feminine, of the American other, then the trope of the narrow *line* would give way to that of the *cross*. The author of *Inundación Castálida* is Sor Juana Inés of the *Cross, musa décima.* The book includes fourteen examples of the ten-line poem, the *décima* from the Latin, *decem,* for "ten." Meters, languages, and styles cross in a poetics of the cross: chiasmus, "placing crosswise," from the Greek letter X, "chi"; and *descussatio,* from the Roman numeral X, the Latin for ten, *decem.* This is a new world of literary miscegenation, one engendered by tropes at work at the convergence of "New World" and "woman." Sor Juana's texts, like "San Pedro Nolasco" and the *Respuesta,* emphasize the crossing of borders. The borders vary. Race is transgressed in "San Pedro Nolasco" and gender in the *Respuesta;* in both there is a similar style of engaged opposites, a common poetics of alterity. For Sor Juana, gender politics informs race politics; it colors the object of representation and the language in which it is written. It is a feminine chiasmus, X, in that conflict along the axis of discursive difference is always a rearticulation of the conflict along the primary axis of gender difference. The various languages, the Spanish, Latin, and Nahuatl of "San Pedro Nolasco," for example, engage in conflicts for presence and authority that replicate the gender conflicts articulated in the *Respuesta.* One slash of the X is always Male/Female; the other can be Spanish/Nahuatl, Villancico/Tocotín, White/Indian; the cross is chiasmus and is always played out in language. And so to the line of the nine muses and their realms, Epic, History, Lyric, Music, Tragedy, Song, Dance, Comedy, and Astronomy, can be added the *musa décima* and the realm of chiasmus.

Sor Juana's chiastic poetics sets writing against the written and enacts a counterhegemonic tactics by writing difference.[11] The *Respuesta* counters the Euro-male, homotextual suppression of the female other, in this case, St. Paul's dictum, *mulieres in ecclesia taceant,* "let women keep silent in church." "San Pedro Nolasco" counters the Eurocentric suppression of racial others, by similarly employing the trope of the cross. These tricks oppose the silencing of the other by articulating marginalized discourses that cross, but do not supplant, the dominant discourse. Such an articulation of difference is characteristically chiastic. Female and male, as well as Spaniard and Mexican, cross and engage in dialogue. There is not the monolineal silencing of the other; instead there is the chiasmus that acknowledges bilineal, *present* differences. In the *Respuesta,* the feminine voice demands presence before the masculist hegemony. In "San Pedro Nolasco," the black and Indian speak in their languages for the first time in the master's church. And even if "San Pedro Nolasco" is read as a white woman's appropriation of the black and Indian slaves' voices, it nevertheless remains clear that Sor Juana argues race and gender similarly. In both, there are the rhetorical tactics, "tricks of the weak," that enact the chiastic tricks that advocate an antisexist and antiracist ideology.

Responsible Tricks

The *Respuesta* is Sor Juana's most fully articulated defense of women; it is her intellectual autobiography, and it is, literally, a *respuesta,* a response to a letter. Its rhetorical tactics, its tricks of engaging repressive logic, have earned the text recognition as the strongest argument by "America's first feminist."[12] It defends the rights of women to write and attacks the injunction that they be silent. It is a letter of response: *La Respuesta a la Muy Ilustre Sor Filotéa de la Cruz,* "Reply to the Very Illustrious Sister Filotéa de la Cruz," responds to a critical letter by the Bishop of Puebla, which he signed with the cross-gendered, feminine pseudonym Sor Filotéa de la Cruz. But if the *Respuesta* is understood as a purely personal defense for her own writing, it is a failure. For after the *Respuesta,* Sor Juana all but ceased writing, writing virtually nothing more before her death.[13]

But the web of responses of the *Respuesta* is much more complex than a simple reply to cross-gendered criticism by the Bishop of Puebla.[14] The first response was Sor Juana's to an old text. She orally criticized the "Sermon on the Mondate," a noted theological treatise originally delivered by the Jesuit Antonio de Vieyra at the Colegio de Lisboa in 1650. Sor Juana's comments had been uttered spontaneously in a conversation, yet an unidentified authority requests that she commit the criticism to paper.[15] Sor Juana's response was to write the *Critique of a Sermon,* which was distributed privately. At some point it came into the possession of the Bishop of Puebla, who had it published. In the process he renamed the *Critique of a Sermon* the *Carta Athenagorica,* thereby transforming the "critique" into a "letter" and making reference to the classical, yet pagan, goddess Athena. He also inserted a preface to the work, a letter addressed to Sor Juana, which he wrote but signed with the feminine pseudonym Sor Filotéa de la Cruz. The bishop's letter, ostensibly written nun to nun, responded critically to Sor Juana's "letters," not just to her criticism of Vieyra but to her writing in general. It is his simultaneously shrouded and official censure that sparks so intense a response in the *Respuesta.* For through Sor Filotéa's letter the bishop asserts authority over the feminine, appropriating a feminine identity and, infinitely more consequential, appropriating, through prescription and circumscription, feminine discourse. The bishop, in the guise of a nun, writes to Sor Juana:

> My Lady: I have seen your letter in which you impugn the favors of Christ as discussed by the Reverend Father, Antonio de Vieyra, in the Sermon on the Mondate. . . . At the very least, I have admired the liveliness of the concepts, the keenness of your proofs, the energetic clarity with which you prove the matter. . . .
>
> So that you may see in this paper's better characters, I have had it printed.
>
> I do not intend to judge, as a strict censor, what may be wrong with your poetry which has been celebrated . . . after that of St. Theresa . . . and other saints, but I wish that as you imitate their meter, you so imitate their choice of subject matter. I do not approve of the vulgarity of those who condemn the use of letters by women, after all so many women have applied themselves to such study, not without the praise of St. Jerome. It is true that St. Paul says that women should not teach. But he does not command that women should not study to know because he only wanted to prevent the risk of insolence in our sex, which is always so given to vanity. . . .
>
> Following this dictum, I do not suggest that you silence your genius by renouncing books, but rather that you better yourself, reading that of Jesus Christ sometime. . . . You have wasted much time studying philosophers and poets . . . your books should im-

prove. What people were more erudite than the Egyptians, who invented the world's first letters? . . . [T]he Egyptians are barbarians . . . all their science strove to perfect the political life of man but did not illustrate how to obtain eternal life: and science that does not illuminate the path to salvation, as everyone knows, God classifies as foolishness. *Science not from the one Crucified is foolishness and mere vanity.*

By this, I do not condemn the reading of those authors, but . . . human letters are slaves that are used to benefiting from the divine; they must be repressed when they steal Divine Wisdom from human reason, making ladies of those destined for servitude.[16]

The bishop's letter vehemently asserts its femininity, from the opening "My Lady," through such posturing as "our sex," to the final signature, *B.L.M. de Umd. su afecta servidora. Philotea de la Cruz,* "Kissing your hand, your affectionate servant, Filotéa de la Cruz." It declares its femininity, a letter written by one woman to another. And yet, Sor Filotéa writes like a man. Her words, we can imagine, articulate those of the bishop, for "she" espouses the very precepts of the Spanish-Catholic patriarchy that codify the hierarchy (literally, the sacred rule) that locates bishop and man above nun and woman.

Sor Juana responds with *La Respuesta a la Muy Ilustre Sor Filotéa de la Cruz*. The *Respuesta* terminates the interplay of authors, and the interplay of authorities, which were set into motion when Sor Juana first responded critically to the "Reverendissimo Padre" Vieyra. The bishop's assumption of authority over Sor Juana's *Critique of a Sermon,* his authorized publication of it as *Carta Athenagorica,* and the authority he asserts over Sor Juana's writing in general are clear indices of gender politics. The authority of the New World woman author is contained and controlled at each exchange with, in every response to, Sor Juana, from the nameless authority's command that she write, to the pseudonymous authority's command that she not.

The contest of authority in the American publication of *Carta Athenagorica* (Puebla, 1690) is similar to the matter of the "tenth muse" in the European publication of the *Inundación Castálida* (Madrid, 1689). The bishop's alignment of Sor Juana with Athena emulates her previous alignment with the muses: the link between poet and goddess confirms an unbroken and straight line of transmission from ancient Greece to imperial Spain.[17] In this scheme, the female poet functions as the requisite intermediary, much as the mother enables the transmission of patrilineal authority. Complicating this trans-temporal, homosocial self-valorization is the fact that not only does the poet reside in the body of a woman but that that body resides in America, in the distant and female continent as well. The inferior-sex/inferior-place status is exploited by the bishop, who authorizes a publication that aggrandizes not only Spanish letters in general but himself as well. Renaming the *Critique of a Sermon* the "Athena-like Letter" generates the same surplus value as does "tenth muse": praise for the New World woman's text praises the praising patriarchal culture and the praising publisher/father. The renaming also operates more insidiously. First of all, it shifts focus away from the act and object of criticism toward a mythical objectification of its writing subject: the praxis of criticizing Vieyra's sermon is supplanted by an ontology of the feminine and Athena-like letter writer. The Athena metaphor itself is equivocal, inscribing "Sor Juana" with both classical wisdom and classical paganism. The latter dimension of Athena supports the shift from critique to letter, for it represents Sor Juana's text as a mere *pagan letter* about Christian theology. Sor Filotéa's negative evaluation of the pre-Christian letters of Egypt was clearly meant to apply to Greek letters too. No matter how erudite Egyptian reason was, it remained "foolishness and mere vanity" precisely because it was pagan. Even when the bishop/nun compares Sor Juana's poetry favorably to that of Christian saints, it comes up short in the most important dimension, "I wish that as you imitate their meter, you so imitate their choice of subject matter." And then there is the matter of the title page. *Carta Athenagorica de la madre Juana Ynes de la Cruz* is supplemented with *que imprime, y dedica a la misma Sor, Phylotea de la Cruz su estudiosa,* so that the text appears coauthored, albeit graciously so. The *Carta Athenagorica* becomes an epistolary anthology, Sor Juana's "letter" and "Sor Filotéa's" letter. The first page of text is the bishop's *imprimatur,* signed Bishop Manuel of Puebla; this is followed by the letter signed Sor Filotéa. Only then does Sor Juana's text appear. The bishop manipulates the text and its authorship, authorizes its publication, and inserts text and an author he authored.

From behind the veil of his transsexual alter ego, the bishop articulates "woman" to woman an implicit command that she refrain from man's work, that she stop writing. "Following this dictum, I do not suggest that you silence your genius by renouncing books" does not censure explicitly; it obscures both authority and command. Explicit censure would mark Filotéa with greater authority than that of a nun and would open the implication to argument. The veiled censure obscures the bishop and works to defer theological debate. In fact, the bishop only alludes to St. Paul's *mulieres in ecclesia taceant* after acknowledging his *bene docentes* "and the women teaching well"; and in so doing, silences objection of a literal following of his dictum. It is a clever piece of rhetoric, one that masks the author, acknowledges the opposing argument, and seemingly undercuts its own authority. Even the bishop's recognition of St. Jerome is significant because Sor Juana's religious order is that of St. Jerome, an order that specifically encourages the education and writing of women. The bishop's articulation of St. Paul through the persona of a nun, "[F]ollowing this dictum, I do not suggest that you silence your genius . . . ," ascribes to his pronouncement a full range of authority and a full complement of perspective. When Sor Filotéa offers "although I do not suggest you stop reading books," it almost sounds as if spoken by an ally, but the negative construction undercuts any sense of positive encouragement. The criticism of "reading books" is particularly misplaced, for Sor Juana's act in *Carta Athenagorica* is not one of reading books, but rather, it is the act of writing criticism. Sor Filotéa's implicit injunction undercuts a much more passive act than Sor Juana's. The bishop's articulation of Saint and nun acknowledges a central tenet of the patriarchal, theological oppression of women, even though the statement has nothing to do with Filotéa's point, that women should read sacred letters. Effectively, by positing the dictum that women should be silent in church, the bishop condemns Sor Juana's act of writing theological criticism in particular and her writing in general.

This appropriation of feminine *author*-ity is the context for Sor Juana's response and informs the text of the *Respuesta*. The topos of *vos me coegistis,* the denial of authorial responsibility, is reiterated in the *Respuesta.* For as Sor Juana states, she wrote very little on her own account but, rather, was *violentada y forzada,* "forced" (with an echo of "violence" and "violation") by *fuerza ajena,* "outside force." She does not articulate with the authority of the unified male subject as does the bishop, and in her representation of racial others, neither do the black nor Indian. Racial and gender others write and speak and are allowed a degree of autonomy to do so, but *fuerzas ajenas* ultimately authorize their articulation. Both the bishop and the anonymous authority are able to appropriate Sor Juana's words because they possess greater power; she is like their colonial subject. The original act of criticizing the theology of the European male priest is permitted, in fact it is authorized, but its articulation is strictly controlled by *fuerzas ajenas.*

But of course she does write. In reaction to all of this, she writes the *Respuesta.* Its rhetorical tactics are simple: to utilize the limited authority allotted the weaker writer and to appropriate the logic of the hegemony, that is, to turn the masculist word back upon itself. These tricks are configured by chiasmus, and assert presence and engagement. The masculist single line of authority is crossed by another line; it is not replaced; both lines are present and active. When the bishop/nun posits *mulieres in ecclesia taceant* to argue that the woman poet should "subordinate profane letters to sacred letters" and *"read* more about Christ Our Lord," Sor Juana responds with a cross:

> How, without Logic could I be apprised of the general and specific way in which the Holy Scripture is Written? How, without Rhetoric, could I understand its figures, its tropes, its locutions? How, without Physics, so many innate questions concerning the nature of animals, their sacrifices, wherein exist so many symbols, many already declared, many still to be discovered? How should I know whether Saul's being refreshed by the sound of David's harp was due to the virtue and natural power of Music, or to a transcendent power God wished to place in David? How, without Arithmetic, could one understand the computations of the years, days, months, hours, those mysterious weeks communicated by Gabriel to Dan-

iel, and others for whose understanding one must know the nature, concordance, and properties of numbers? How, without Geometry, could one measure the Holy Arc of the Covenant and the Holy City of Jerusalem, whose mysterious measures are foursquare in their dimensions, as well as the miraculous proportions of all their parts? How, without Architecture, could one know the great Temple of Solomon, of which God Himself was the Author who conceived the disposition and the design, and the Wise King but the overseer who executed it, of which temple there was no foundation without mystery, no column without symbolism, no cornice without allusion, nor architrave without significance; and similarly others of its parts, of which the least fillet was never intended solely for the service and complement of Art, but as symbol of greater things? How, without great knowledge of the laws and parts of which History is comprised, could one understand historical Books? . . . How, without great erudition, could one apprehend the secular histories of which the Holy Scripture makes mention, such as the many customs of the Gentiles, their many rites, their many ways of speaking? (34–6)

Such is the cross of Sor Juana. She assumes the bishop's discourse: she does not refute the logic of the religious doctrine nor its authority; she does not oppose the authoritative *line* of thought. And to the degree to which she acknowledges that authority, she espouses the Euro-male homosocial discourse.[18] But her argument is much more complex than that; it is, perhaps, too subtle for the bishop to grasp. Her heterotext crosses his line with another.

The tactics of the *Respuesta* are the chiastic trick. Sor Juana appropriates the authoritative discourse but employs it to prove the bishop wrong. She does not reject the hegemony's semantics, logic, nor authority, but rearticulates them in a different style, in another line of thought. So configured, this alternate alignment asserts an alternate semantics. She crosses the authoritative, male-to-male line and the logic of self-reference and tautology with a relativizing, female line and a *chi*-logic of presence and engagement. The bishop's use of St. Paul's *mulieres in ecclesia taceant* is clear, even if uttered through the fiction of Sor Filotéa: male utterance constitutes male authority. When she uses the quote, Sor Juana does not question its authority, but she does rearticulate it and writes, literally, from the body of a woman. This feminine locus is both appropriation and realignment of the Euro-male homosocial metonymy; the feminine articulation crosses the male at the point of silence in church. She authorizes her own authority as author through the troping that connects and opposes by chiastic trick, by speaking like a woman speaking like a man.

And Sor Juana also responds to the bishop in the *Respuesta* as a woman speaking to a woman. Sor Juana frequently addresses Sor Filotéa as "my lady" and writes as if she were addressing a confidant, another nun. It is as if Sor Juana discusses the world of women in passages of feminine discourse; her scientific observations in the kitchen are one example. There is clear irony aimed at the bishop in her so repeated woman-to-woman rhetorical coloring. This is perhaps sharpest in her discussion of men. For she expresses a very ladylike disdain for contact with men. Nun to nun, Sor Juana explains her entry into the convent *para la total negación que tenía al matrimonio,* "because of my complete opposition to marriage." She carries this disdain further, appropriating the Church's vision of sin in female and male contact. She turns Filotéa's argument back upon itself with another chiastic trick:

> For I do not find that the custom of men teaching women is without its peril, lest it be in the severe tribunal of the confessional, or from the remote decency of the pulpit, or in the distant learning of books – never in the personal contact of immediacy. And the world knows this is true; and, notwithstanding, it is permitted solely from the want of learned elder women. Then is it not detrimental, the lack of such women? The question should be addressed by those who bound to that *Let women keep silence in the church,* say that it is blasphemy for women to learn and teach, as if it were not the Apostle himself who said: *The aged women . . . teaching well.*

Filotéa's use of *mulieres in ecclesia taceant* comes back to undermine the bishop's strategy, for St. Paul also recognizes women teachers. And as Sor Juana argues that the bishop's discourse argues, women should teach women, and to "know" religion, it is necessary to "know" the profane. Yet despite the efficacy of Sor Juana's chiastic tricks, in her appropriation of the masculist discourse and articulation as a woman, the *Respuesta* comes up short as prescriptive writing. It is, after all, virtually the last thing she writes.

The protofeminism which is most clearly delineated in the *Respuesta* had an impact on her other writing as well. For her relationship to masculist authority prefigures Sor Juana's representations of racial alterity. Her woman's body and woman's words and the tactics she employs to counter misogynist suppression set the pattern for her reading and writing American others.

Her Self and Others

The "Villancicos San Pedro Nolasco" was included in *Inundación Castálida* but was originally published as a single volume in 1677. It problematizes race and language politics in a manner similar to Sor Juana's problematizing of gender relations. "San Pedro Nolasco" and "Asunción" both represent two marginalized American others: Pilico, an Afro-Hispanic slave, and an unnamed Indian.[19] The black and Indian are represented, that is, given presence in the text, and both are given voice in the style in which they speak. For Sor Juana's representation of these American others incorporates the representation of their speech styles. Not only are they *present* in a context that normally excludes them, they *speak* in languages not normally printed. This representation of racial alterity follows the style of Sor Juana's representation of gender alterity: both are manifested in discursive crossing.

Villancicos are laudatory verses, literally sung in church on the day of the saint they praise. The series of eight villancicos that comprises "San Pedro Nolasco" was performed at matins on January 31, 1677. In writing sound and sense, Sor Juana took the opportunity to recontextualize the life of the saint and to interject local *son et lumière* in the process. Nolasco is the slave's saint: in the thirteenth century, he spent his fortune ransoming Christian captives, that is, buying slaves, from Moors in Catalonia. Sor Juana delineates the life of the French saint;

but she does not stop there, she seizes the opportunity to link the Old
World slavery in Nolasco's time with the New World slavery in her
own time. The eighth and final villancico offers criticism from two
New World slaves, a black and an Indian. The villancicos cross over
from praise for the Old World male to criticism by the New World
male by way of the New World woman writer. The seven villancicos
end with a final testimony to Nolasco, a striking chiasmus that undercuts the lines of praise:

que, como era buen Francés,

del mal francés los curaba.

"Since he was a good Frenchman, he would cure them from French
illness," that is, from syphilis. Venereal disease appears fifteen lines
from the end of the seven villancicos attesting to Nolasco's venerable
status. It appears in the chiastic cross of *buen Francés* with *mal francés*. In
one sense, the *mal francés* anticipates the eighth villancico, which is the
"Ensaladilla," that is, the "salad" of disparate and comic voices, for
there is humor in the crossing of the euphemism. In another sense,
however, the *mal francés* infects the image of the *buen Francés*. Those
lines, after all, are the conclusion of the "serious" villancicos.

The serious praise for Nolasco is further undercut by the second
line of the chiasmus. The first line of the X links *buen Francés* with *mal
francés,* and the second links *como era* with *curaba*. The first asserts irony
of sense and similarity of sound: it is the play of difference and similarity that makes the line between *buen Francés* and *mal francés* work, that
makes it humorous and cutting. At first, the second line seems to
function only formally: the sound of the trisyllabic *como era* resonates
with the sound of *curaba*. But the line chiasmus draws from *como era,*
"since he was," to *curaba,* "he would cure," can be read in a variety of
ways. Chiasmus formally inserts *como* (of *como era*) and *cura* (of *curaba*)
into the new syntax *como cura*. The new line, *como cura,* can then be
read as either "since/how he cures" or, significantly, "like a priest."
The pun almost works in English too: "cures" nearly replicates "cu-
rate." The sense of *como cura* as "like a priest" is supplemented by

other possible chiastic readings: *como era cura* translates as "since he was a priest," and *como cura va (cura va* pronounced the same as *curaba)* translates as "as the priest goes." Chiasmus, then, constructs two new syntactical arrangements and then crosses them. It constructs new meanings as when the ironic line of "venerable Frenchman and venereal disease" is crossed by a line that reads "like a priest," "since he was a priest," and "as the priest goes."[20] The second line undercuts the irony of the first, and the link of priest and disease is rendered literal. But the chiasmus has it both ways at once: the "serious" veneration coexists with the venereal contamination of man and profession.

In the final villancico, Nolasco remains the object of a praise of sorts, yet new characters participate in a comic-critique, in dialogues among colonial subjects who are literally a world apart. A complex interplay of languages, discourses, and styles radically shifts the focus of "San Pedro Nolasco" from the religious-historical Old World to the social realities of seventeenth-century Mexico. For brought into the church to conclude the praise of the slave's redeemer are the New World slave and colonial subject, black and Indian. They sing slaves' songs in the words and rhythms of conquered peoples. The eighth villancico is the "Ensaladilla," a mixture of sounds and styles; it is also the one villancico that crosses the other seven.[21] It crosses the authoritative discourse by representing the word and body of the racial other.

This final villancico is divided into three sections, each of which is prefaced by the poet-narrator in literary Spanish. The first section, "Puerto Rico," comprises estribillo and coplas in the Afro-Spanish speech of the Caribbean slave. This is followed by the so-called "Dialogue," the failed attempt at communication across class, between a pompous Latin-speaking student and an uneducated Spanish-speaking man. Finally, the "Tocotín" concludes "San Pedro Nolasco"; it is an interlingual, Spanish-Nahuatl, version of the tocotín, a combination of indigenous poetry, song, and dance.[22] The interlingualism of "Puerto Rico" and "Tocotín" provides the linguistic shift that Americanizes and updates "San Pedro Nolasco." The style of the "Ensaladilla" forces a reconsideration of slavery by extrapolating Nolasco to a New World context. The presence and utterance of Pilico, like that of the Indian, interjects alterity into the "sacred letters sung at

matins," that is, into the Eurocentric, homosocial, self-valorizing rit-
ual. And this is very like the chiastic trick of realigning *mulieres in
ecclesia taceant* in the *Respuesta*. The "Ensaladilla" crosses with "Puerto
Rico," "Tocotín," and "Dialogue" so that "San Pedro Nolasco" is
crosshatched by lines of race and class.

  "Puerto Rico" is striking. Pilico's language must have shaken up
the mass at matins on January 31, 1677. For after seven traditional
villancicos praising Nolasco, the singing of the nuns in the cathedral
was crossed by a black slave whose words and rhythms and body had
not figured in such services before:

> ¡Tumba, la-lá-la; tumba, la-lé-le;
> que donde ya Pilico, escrava no quede!
> ¡Tumba, tumba, la-lé-le; tumba, la-lá-la;
> que donde ya Pilico, no quede escrava!

"Wherever Pilico is, no slave remains" chants Pilico to what could be
the Ur-salsa rhythm and in words born of the culture clash of Amer-
ica. His Spanish is Africanized: *escrava* for *esclava*, *ya* for *está*, *Pilico* for
Perico. His *metro* and *estilo* enact difference. The sense of his speech is
equally striking. Pilico criticizes the religion and race that enslave him:

> They say that they redeem,
> but it seems like trickery,
> I say I live at the factory
> but the priests never save me.
>   The other night with my woman
> I couldn't sleep and started to think
> that Nolasco doesn't like dark folk
> the way he likes his whites.
>   He only redeems Spaniards,
> but God, here's the trap:
> though black, we're still human,
> even if they do call us beasts!

Pilico quite explicitly denounces racism, and does so in Afro-Spanish
dialect and in 1677.

  "San Pedro Nolasco" ends with the unique combination of *metro, idioma y estilo* of the tocotín. As with Pilico, the Indian's sound and sense seem remarkably out of place. The Indian's language combines Spanish and Nahuatl in the interplay of the intercultural colonized subject. His language mirrors the conflicts embodied in colonial relations. The oddity of his presence in both villancico and church signifies his marginalization in Eurocentric consciousness. The Indian begins in doubt:

> Los Padres bendito
> > tiene ò Redemptor;
> > *amo nic neltoca*
> > *quemati no Dios.*
> Sólo Dios *Pilzintli*
> > del Cielo baxò,
> > y nuestro *tlatlácol*
> > nos lo perdonò.
> Pero estos *Teopixqui*
> > dice en so sermón
> > que este San Nolasco
> > *miechtin* compró.

> [The blessed fathers
> > have a redeemer,
> > I don't believe it
> > I know my God.
> Only God's dear son
> > descended from Heaven
> > and forgave us
> > our sins
> But these priests
> > say in their sermon
> > that this Saint Nolasco
> > bought them all.]

The unnamed Indian continues and concludes the whole series of villancicos with an affirmation of the faith: he wants to buy a redeemer like Saint Pedro Nolasco. It is an odd affirmation that follows his original reticence at accepting the praise for Nolasco, yet it is an affirmation of sorts. The odd acceptance of Nolasco, that is, the Indian's desire to purchase him, at once belies the Indian's faith (he is an idolater) and Nolasco's stature (he is a commodity) yet, ironically, is in accord with Nolasco's practice of buying others.

The discursive styles of Pilico and the Indian are similar in that they mix languages, but differ in the levels of that mixing. For Pilico *escrava* signals the Africanization of Spanish, but he speaks Spanish. His is variation within one national language. For the Indian, however, *quemati no Dios* demonstrates a linguistic crossing between national languages.[23] The difference in styles could well point to differences in Eurocentric conceptions of Pilico and the Indian with regard to *nation,* that is, conceptions of a country-less black and a Mexican colonial subject. Both styles, however, assert alternate presence and engage through difference. The marginalized other's presence is manifested in the form of the expression; Afro–America and Native America engage Spain in the play of words. This interlingualism reflects, of course, the more general interculturalism at play in colonial America. Pilico and the Indian's words articulate linguistic mestizajes that emerge in the broad context of cultural and racial mestizaje. But the backdrop for their linguistic interplay, as it is manifested by the nun's pen, is a pervasive bilingualism that informs a bi-gendered world view. The black and Indian (and feminine) discourses cross a Latin and Spanish bilingualism because the line of authority from Rome to Spain to New Spain is written in those two languages. Latin and Spanish are the languages of Church and State, of religion and empire. Latin always exists as the etymological and theological backdrop to Spanish, and, significantly, Latin is gendered: it is the language of patriarchal authority; it is the language that constitutes that authority. It is the Latin, *mulieres in ecclesia taceant,* that writes the ethical suppression of women. And it is in Spanish that the two slaves come to be *negro, indio,* and *esclavo.* In this way the tricks of race crossing in "San Pedro Nolasco" replicates the tricks of gender crossing in the *Respuesta.* In both cases Spanish and Latin are the languages of authority; they constitute race and gender power relations. Sor Juana's chiastic tricks function similarly with regard to race and gender: in both cases they do not deny the Eurocentric patriarchal authority, but they do cross it discursively; they do cross it critically.

The form of the content of slave utterance and feminine utterance is similar too. Both the *Respuesta* and "San Pedro Nolasco" interject the (sub)altern into the consciousness of the hegemony by the appropriation and rearticulation of the authoritative discourse. The woman crosses the male in arguing for her right to write; the black and the Indian cross the Catholic colonist in doubting his and her religious authority. And it is relatively *her* authority too. Both Pilico and the Indian are represented by the criollo woman; there is no question of their self-presentation; she *author*-izes their words. And eventually, the radicalism of their speech is undercut by what their words say. Ultimately, Sor Juana supports the colonist religion. And in missionary form, she authorizes Pilico and the Indian's recanting. While both may have doubted, both recapitulate: Pilico declares that the devil made him doubt; the Indian wants to buy a saint who bought Christian slaves. The text opposes racism, but it clearly supports Catholicism. Perhaps the key to understanding this lies in "Catholicism," in the claims of "universality" of the Roman Catholic Church and the Spanish Empire. In this "catholic" sense, simultaneous and noncontradictory pleas could well be made for the recognition of difference and for the acknowledgment of the authorities of the church (over the soul) and empire (over the body).[24]

And yet it is worth considering to what degree Sor Juana's texts espouse colonialism. In the first place, the context of the performance of the villancicos, matins in church, offers limited opportunity for radical discourse. In this sense, the performances of Pilico and the Indian, as well as the *mal francés,* seem radical enough. If contemporary readers of the *Respuesta* can be cautioned in the introduction to ignore the passive tone of its opening in order to recognize a truer radicalism, then perhaps a similar reading could apply to "San Pedro Nolasco" as well. And even if we were to downplay other factors contrasting "San Pedro Nolasco" with the *Respuesta,* factors such as her relative age at authorship, twenties versus forties, or the problem of representing others compared to self, there are still the common chiastic tactics that demand consideration. It is true that slave and colonized subject ultimately *say* they embrace the one true faith and recognize the single line of authority, but they say it in the interplay of languages that crosses that single line. And it is true that Sor Juana says she acknowledges *mulieres in ecclesia taceant,* but she says it in a cross of protofeminist discourse. There is no erasure of black or Indian or woman. And while none of their voices supplants the dominant, each engages it, crosses the line of authority. Sor Juana does not seek to erase the hegemony, and she remains ardently Catholic. After the *Respuesta* she writes three affirmations of faith and signs one of them in her own blood. For her, Christ is the *chi* of the chiasmus, the *Xmus,* the point of convergence, the point of articulation where other lines can cross. For me, Sor Juana is the point on the line of cultural transmission crossed by the body and the words of a woman.

Nation and States

Net Laguna

Je voudrais dormir au bord du lac,
al lado de este que en inglés es lack,
to sleep beside lo que je voudrais,
junto al lago peut-être nager.

Je voudrais dormir in the wide aire
mentir in the cut, herida mía;
avoir des rêves al revés de anger,
rage, où nagent les anges d'argent,
rien, and rain entero peace of time.

To ask la cuna of first, ¿qué es, pez?
Passé pescado, sin essense, pecado original,
con d'aillures de l'essence un seul poisson,
the poison sol au bord laguna cut water
corps de l'eau, de l'heure, and the fold que eres.

Une tranche de la vie, flesh bits, minutiae,
¿qu'a bu qui a vu qué ha visto l'año que entra quién?

An Other Tongue

When I write about Chicano poetry, one of the first examples that comes to mind is José Montoya's "El Louie." I'm sure this is so because the poem strikes me as being thoroughly Chicano. It is, after all, about the high life and tragic end of Louie Rodríguez, exemplar of urban youth subculture; it is an elegy for a pachuco. And outside Chicano barrios, there exists nothing quite like the pachuco. Louie would dance both mambo and boogie, and conflate the cultures from both sides of the border.

Yet more vital than Louie's story for me, as a poet and critic, is the language of Louie's story. And the language of "El Louie" matches its content: the verse is as thoroughly Chicano as is Louie's life. It begins, "Hoy enterraron al Louie / and San Pedro o sanpinche / are in for it . . ." [loosely, Today they buried Louie / and heaven or hell / are in for it . . .]. "El Louie" mixes languages in the style of popular Chicano speech: there is Spanish, there is English, and there is hybridization.

This style of multilingual hybridization is pushed to the extreme in a poem by José Antonio Burciaga. "Poema en tres idiomas y caló" delineates the linguistic tensions embodied in the Chicano and is written in an interplay of languages, Spanish, English, Nahuatl, and the Chicano hybridization, caló. Each of which is present in the following two lines: "Mi mente spirals al mixtli, / buti suave I feel cuatro lenguas in mi boca" [My mind spirals to the clouds, / so smooth I feel four tongues in my mouth]. "Poema en tres idiomas y caló" acknowledges the style of Chicano discourse and reflects the intercultural dynamics at play in constructing Chicano identity. For, being for Chicanos occurs in the interface between Anglo and Latin America, on the border that is not so much a river from the Gulf of Mexico to El Paso and a wire fence from there to the Pacific but, rather, a much broader area where human interchange goes beyond the simple "American or no" of the border check. It is the space to contest cultural identities more complex than the more facile questions of legal status or images in popular culture.

"El Louie" and "Poema en tres idiomas y caló" are born of a linguistic interplay that finds its central analog in the porous frontier. Mexicans negotiate the border like no others, north and south, south and north, realizing simultaneous cultural fission and fusion. It is this border context that differentiates the styles of linguistic interplay of Chicano poetry from other styles of polyglot poetics. The poetry of Eliot and Pound, for example, incorporates other languages, from the Italian of Dante, to German conversation, to Chinese characters. The poetics of Montoya and Burciaga is similar to Eliot and Pound's in the fact of its linguistic hybridization, but the fact of the border contributes to a different emphasis in the styles of that multilingualism. In Eliot and Pound there is much greater emphasis on quotation and literary allusion; while in Montoya and Burciaga, poetic hybridization tends to replicate the polyglot style of quotidian Chicano discourse. The former often focuses on the content of that form (for example, Dante's *Inferno*) and interlards "significant" texts; the later focuses on the form of that form (for example, caló, hybridization itself) and implements discursive interaction.[1]

Because Chicano verse actualizes the discourse of the border and embraces a broad range of difference, comparing the styles of linguistic interplay becomes a prime method of considering Chicano poetics. One way that the styles of interplay can be compared is by juxtaposing the sizes of the linguistic units that play in the works of various authors.[2] That is, from the macro to the micro, the monolingual unit ranges from genres; to texts; to poetic and grammatical units; to individual words; and to morphemes, phonemes, and graphemes. Lucha Corpi, for example, differentiates language at the level of genre: poetry is Spanish (*Palabras de mediodía* and *Variaciones sobre un tempestad* are two collections), novels are English (*Delia's Song* and *Eulogy for a Brown Angel*). For the poet Juan Felipe Herrera, the monolingual unit tends to be the book. *Rebozos of Love* and *Akrilica* are primarily Spanish books, while *Exiles of Desire* and *Facegames* are

English. Barbara Brinson Curiel (*Speak to Me From Dreams*) and Francisco X. Alarcón (*Cuerpo en Llamas* and *Snake Poems*) tend to vary language within the book, so that the monolingual unit is the poem, the stanza, or the phrase. Both José Montoya and José Antonio Burciaga alternate languages within the verse line and even within the individual word. In "El Louie," the word *shinadas* is a hybrid of English and Spanish, the English verb *to shine* is written as a Spanish past participle. This hybridization is a type of double voicing, as in "Poema en tres idiomas y caló," where Nahuatl infuses Spanish (*loco* becomes *locotl*) and English (*English* becomes *Englishic*). In Alurista's *Nationchild Plumaroja*, even the typeface speaks difference: the poems are printed in the script of barrio graffiti.

Border discourse contextualizes Chicano poetry to such an extent that even essentially monolingual verse is read within the larger framework of a multilingual poetics. Lorna Dee Cervantes's *Emplumada* is basically an English book, although it does have one Spanish-language poem and Spanish words and phrases in others. Yet against the relative English consistency is manifested a subject matter of intercultural conflict. And it is a Spanish title that effects the unifying tropes of the text: *Emplumada*, that is, pen, feather, pen flourish, plumage. Even very monolingual texts, such as Lucha Corpi's *Palabras de mediodía* and Bernice Zamora's *Restless Serpents,* are read as Chicano texts at the extremes of Chicano discourse but not beyond. Because the degree to which the discourse is polyglot, another language is implied, and such discourse imbues *Palabra* and *Serpent* with internal dialogue.

The border as discursive and existential fact does something to the interpretation of Chicano writing. It removes the discussion of the styles of linguistic interplay from the realm of the aesthetic alone because the border is a space where English and Spanish compete for presence and authority. It is not the site of mere either/or linguistic choice but one of quotidian linguistic conflict where the utterance is born at home in English and in Spanish and in caló. Here, verse is born of and sustained on conflict that has real world consequence. In the broad interface between Anglo and Latin America, the operative tropes, the definitions, the histories and logics and legal codes, the semantics and the epistemes are contested daily. Because of this, the study of literary style is inextricably bound up with that of discursive practice. And as Chicano discourse demarcates the realm of the poem, so it does the Chicano subject. Chicanismo occurs in the very nexus of languages and is continually marked by utterances in the linguistic borderlands.

In poem and in daily speech, English and Spanish bestow different levels of authority on text and speaker. The relative imbalance in authority grows daily in the present era of increasing legislative suppression of languages other than English. English carries with it the status of authorization by the hegemony. It is the language of Anglo America and of linguistic Anglo-Americans, whether or not they be ethnic Anglos. Further, it is the language of the greatest military and economic power in the world. Spanish is a language of Latin Americans, south of the border and north. Across the border, Spanish is a Third World language; here it is the language of the poor.

Today as I write in Santa Cruz, California, the local newspaper carries an article that illustrates contemporary linguistic relations in the United States. It is an interesting variant to an otherwise common story in Chicano neighborhoods: the story of deportation. The article begins, "School and city officials expressed outrage, this week over the Border Patrol's arrest of three Hispanic students outside an English as a Second Language class." Needless to say, the three were deported to Mexico. They were denied presence in "America" while trying to learn "American." Reading this from my Chicano perspective, I am struck by the irony of it: irony, not only that "officials expressed outrage" at so typical an INS action, but irony also that the story made it into print in the first place.[3] For we have been trained to know that, despite the fact that we make up perhaps one in four in the state, what Mexicans, Chicanos, and Latinos say and do in our language is not worthy of print.

To speak, or even to attempt to learn to speak, sparks a display of power from the dominant group. It is within this system of unequal discursive relationships that Chicanos speak and write. This is evident, institutionally, in examples that range from the sixteen states that are officially English only, to the four English national language bills introduced into Congress *last year,* to the American Academy of Poets policy that the national Walt Whitman award be for English-only verse. And from the Congress to the academy to the streets, over and over, incessantly, an unequal struggle goes on in which Anglo America strives to inhibit dialogue, marginalize chicanismo, and silence other tongues, and by synecdoche, silence other people.

But the United States is not a space where homogeneous speakers articulate a single language. It is, rather, the site of polyglossia, where multiple national languages interact. English is neither the sole nor original language. Yet U.S. American culture presents itself as an English-language culture; it espouses a single-language ethos; it strives very actively to assert a monolingual identity. This is to say, its overriding tendency is toward the assertion of a monolingual authority and the complementary suppression of alternate languages. In Bakhtin's terms, this tendency is monologic, espousing the monologue of a dominant, authoritative discourse, eschewing dialogue with others. This monologic bias, from the English Only movement to the writing of U.S. history, valorizes English and suppresses expression both in and about Spanish.[4] English is elevated from the status of one language among languages, albeit the dominant one, to that of sole and pervasive language in general. This is coupled with the simultaneous erasure of Spanish through the restriction of its use and the interdiction of dialogue.

Because internal dialogue is so contributing a factor in the making of Chicano discourse, the dynamics of language are especially foregrounded in the verse and in the subjectification of the Chicano. Both come to be within a matrix that includes English, Spanish, and caló. This matrix, which Bakhtin calls heteroglossia, is the context of historical, interlingual, and interdiscursive factors that come into play in, and affect the meaning of, any utterance. Chicano poem and cultural subject acknowledge heteroglossia; this is what Chicano means: intercultural heteroglot. "American," according to the Anglo-American's selective application of the continental name, means the suppression of heteroglossia and the selective recognition of only that set and sequence of factors that enhance the self and mark the alterity of others. Distinctions of language, color, and religion are but some of the markers employed to subjugate. For Chicanos, linguistic practice has been the legal criteria to classify, to differentiate: Spanish Speaking, Spanish Surnamed, White Hispanic. Chicano subjectification is never far from the competition among languages.

The role of discursive activity in the creation and maintenance of identity can be neither disinterested nor indifferent. Each articulation is a taking of sides and a demarcation of subjects. There can be no objective disinterest within a situation of constantly unequal subjectification, for even to choose not to choose tacitly supports the status quo. It is comparable to the border check point question, "American or no?" Anything other than a prompt "yes," even a slight pause, causes suspicion and casts the American status of the speaker in doubt. For Chicanos it is patently clear: each utterance and textual manifestation identifies and aligns, promulgating one version of self, one dimension of space.[5]

So what does the Chicano discourse, does the Chicano poem do? First, in the common senses of language use, other than poetry, the mere presence of Chicano discourse resists Anglo-American suppression of heteroglossia, much as the background noise of menials jars a social gathering. The presence of difference undermines the aspiration for an English-only ethos. And inasmuch as Chicano discourse is specifically multilingual and multivoiced, it further undermines the tendency toward single-language and single-voiced monologue, that is, it undermines Anglo-American monologism. It undercuts claims of prevalence, centrality, and superiority, and confirms the condition of heteroglossia. It draws the monologue into dialogue. In short, it dialogizes the authoritative discourse.

And the poem? It is often maintained that poetry is a personal form of discourse, the particular discursive act of an individual poet. Bakhtin argued a generic distinction, that poetry was formally monologic, the single-voiced discourse (*edinogolosnoe slovo*) of the individual poet.[6] He felt that it could not articulate the double-voiced discourse (*dvugolosnoe slovo*) of the polyglot novel. Bakhtin eventually reduced the absoluteness of his epic/novel differentiation, yet he nevertheless maintained that it was novelistic discourse that enabled the dialogues among social discourses, as well as that between character and author.

But clearly there is a tradition of poetry that is, at least in form, multilingual. Eliot and Pound emphasize the content of that form in the creation of poetic pastiche in poems that blend polyglot quotation and allusion with lines of English language, modernist verse. Eliot's quoting Dante, for example, by the simple fact of including Italian, does make for a bilingual poetry, and one that is, in a sense, double-voiced. But to the extent that the work is resonant with the authoritative discourse, whether it be Anglo-Catholic Royalist or Mussolini Fascist, such bilingualism is not disharmonious with English or Italian nationalist tendency toward single-voiced monologism. This is to say that in this fashion, literary citation and allusion function in a manner that does not oppose the national narratives; indeed, such literary hybridization functions as a self-referential and tautological affirmation of the national telos: the hailing of the great dead establishes the continuity of cultural transmission to the latter day.[7]

This, I realize, is a generalization that here only serves to contrast a very different poetics undertaken by Montoya and Burciaga; it ignores completely, for example, Eliot or Pound's incorporation of common and quotidian speech. Nevertheless, it remains obvious that the two Chicano poets do not cite in the same manner but instead implement an interlingual style that emphasizes the form of the form. Their caló is multilingual and double-voiced in its eclectic hybridization. Its style opposes standard English and opposes the canonical literary telos. It conflicts with the authoritative discourse; it is dialogic. It is in this sense that the simple contrast of styles is possible.[8] The strategy of Eliot and Pound can be understood to emphasize the selective drawing from the treasure house of texts central to Western culture, texts that constitute the authoritative discourse. The strategy of Montoya and Burciaga can be understood to emphasize the style of linguistic hybridization of the present-day border context, hybridization that dialogizes the Anglo-American monologue. That Chicano poetry upsets the authoritative lines of American literature and of the American self makes for a type of poetry that requires the consideration of the discourse and power relations that form its context.

The study of discursive practices that specifically subjugate and subjectify colonized peoples overlaps with Bakhtin's more general work in the shared focus on the work of language by which one group fashions authority over another. It specifically examines the process of subject formation within the context of a gross imbalance of power. The relationships between Britain and India or between Britain and Ireland, for example, are overdetermined by colonial contexts. Still today, the colonial language, English, figures prominently in the construction of Indian and of Irish identities. Colonial discursive practices are more immediately tied to displays of physical power than are the literary discursive practices that Bakhtinian analysis is usually employed to describe. Each colonial situation is unique, yet common to all are the conquest and domination of one people by another and a dominant, monologic discourse whose employment is linked to violence.

Colonial discourse criticism applied to internal U.S. relations would make manifest that the Chicano is *identified* as other for the United States. The subjectification of the Chicano occurs within the context of an Anglo-American domination that assigns marginality as a constitutive component. Within that context, each speech act is perlocutionary and differentiates in the act of uttering. The Chicano subject is marginal because the signifier and signified "chicano" are marginalized in Anglo-American discourse. The sign "chicano" and the subject "chicano" are made alien by the centripetal forces of monologism that strive to locate the self at the center and to locate the other at the margins. The other is contained, linguistically and spatially, on reservations, in barrios, in the colonies, far from the centers of the colonizer's self and home and female body. "Chicano" exists, to the limited extent that it does exist, as a marker of difference, of inferiority and alterity. Being "chicano" is a process of continual remaking, a discursive process that is always negotiated within the context of the circumscribing discursive practices of the United States.

Any monologism, with its drive toward a unitary and self-refle(x/ct)ive discourse, discriminates self from other, but in the colonial situation, it radically differentiates the identities of colonizer and colonized. The extreme power differential prescribes literal subjectification through regimentation of semantics and prescribes physical subjugation through regimentation of the body. The colonizer's language and discourse are elevated to the status of arbiter of truth and reality; the world comes to be as the authoritative discourse says. For discursive practice does not simply represent colonialism after the fact but functions as the means to order colonial relations and to establish the meaning of those relations, in short, to define the world for the benefit of the colonizer. It is this absoluteness of authority in the face of alternate discourses and other peoples that characterizes colonial relationships, relationships such as those between English and Irish, between Anglo-American and Sioux, between white and black South African.[9]

The dominant discourse has such authority that it becomes adopted, in varying degrees, by the colonized subject. What begins during the conquest, in precolonialism, as an externally imposed representation becomes in colonialism per se and in postcolonialism a self-imposed subjectification. The marginal other autocolonizes himself and herself each time the hegemonic discourse is articulated. The utterance of English in Ireland or the use of a British-styled school system in India reinforces daily the colonizer's presence in the heart of the colonized. The authoritative discourse is, after all, a prescribed monologue structured to inhibit dialogue with the natives. Who would read these lines I now write, if they were written in caló? According to the monologue, the colonized subject is homogeneous and static, a silent text that can be written and read but never talked with. For this subject, discourse is itself textualized, a codified set of relationships and prescribed responses that delimit a fixed reality. The colonized subject becomes the (sub)altern other prescribed by the dominant discourse in the act of articulating that discourse. The other comes to be according to, and illustrates the validity of, an externally constructed social text.

Autocolonialism is perhaps most marked in those situations where the colonist never goes home, that is, in internal colonialism. In the United States, "internal colonialism" was first employed in the 1960s to describe the "colonization" of black Americans in white America.[10] Black nationalists and social scientists used it to describe a situation analogous to the colonial except that the colonized space was permanently encompassed by the colonizer space, that is, the colonist never left the colony. Within the confines of the United States, American Indians, Chicanos, and Puerto Ricans share the experience of conquest and continued occupation by Anglo America; blacks represent that special conquest, the forced immigration of the slave. None were originally English speakers.[11] But for them, after the decimation of conquest, enslavement or genocide, the acceptance of the colonizer's linguistic practices has translated into an increase in life span and perceived human worth and a decrease in lynching and forced sterilization. The discursive relationships that constitute internal colonies are similar to those that constitute external colonies; the methods that describe the discursive processes that have subjugated and subjectified Indian, Irish, Algerian, and Aztec are methods that can illuminate the processes of internal colonialism within the United States.

In response to colonialism, there are several general reactions available for the colonized other. Very generally, the reactions can be described according to different criteria as autocolonial, nationalist, or hybrid, on the one hand, or as monologic or dialogic, on the other. The former describes the difference between the colonized's and the colonizer's discourse; the latter describes the relative tendency to engage in dialogue. Autocolonialism, in the extreme, requires the other's adoption of the hegemonic discourse to the extent that the colonizer permits and to the extent that the other is able to predicate it. The other assimilates both discourse and the relationships it systematizes, so to the degree the discourse suppresses, the autocolonist effaces or denigrates him/herself from within. In the endeavor to mimic the monologue of power, the other harmonizes with it and suppresses difference. Autocolonialism discourages dialogue. It is monologic.

Nationalism opposes the authority of the colonial discourse with the authority of an alternate discourse. Nationalist discourse defines itself in the related actions of rejecting the externally imposed system of representation and advancing an indigenous one. The alien, colonially defined world is rejected in favor of the native, nationalistically defined world. The articulation of difference would seem to dehegemonize colonial authority by its presence alone, and in a sense it does do this. The move to *select* one discourse over another is dialogic, but the content of that selection, the nationalist monologue, is monologic. Nationalism *combines* native elements into a privileged discourse, deaf (*gluxoj*), as Bakhtin would say, to a deaf colonial discourse. Their "dialogue" is the clash of senseless monologues. Its overriding tendency is monologic.

Hybridization, or cultural mestizaje, differs from both autocolonialism and nationalism in that it is inherently polyglot. Hybridized discourse rejects the principle of monologue and composes itself by selecting from competing discourses. Further, there is no detritus of difference; distinct elements remain so, relating in a dialogue of dissimilarity. Hybridization asserts dialogue by articulating an alternate discourse and by organizing itself in internal dialogue. It is born of the struggles for discursive dominance and relates within itself and with other discourses according to the principle of dialogue. It is dialogic because it is so multivoiced.

The discursive actions, which authorize colonialism's stringent monologue and extreme power displacement, prescribe antithesis as the ordering factor of differentiation. Antithesis engenders a propitious rhetoric of difference that opposes the favorable representation of one people to the radical marginalization of a homogeneous and alien other. Colonial and monologic discourse transpires through the rhetorical fashioning of what, from the dominant viewpoint, is a fortuitous reality. There can be no objective, disinterested discourse in colonial relationships.

Antithetical subjectification and radical differentiation are rhetorically determined as the dominant group employs its available discourses (for example, science, religion, law, art) in order to constitute, codify, and read its literal power. Scientific discourse has been used to quantify and qualify, to prove (empirically or logically, for example) the *essentially* different nature of the other. Examples range from the Victorian biologists' fetishization of the female, especially black female, buttocks and genitals,[12] to the more contemporary gender and racial discrimination through ostensibly objective intelligence testing. Religious discourse defines the good and the bad, the right and the wrong. Even in seemingly moderate form, it identifies the heathen and heretic, and is typically employed in the rhetoric of genocide, be it of Jews or Armenians this century, or of American Indians before. The law, of course, defines citizen, alien, slave and constrains woman, child, Indian. Presently, it determines who is countable in the census and what languages can be spoken at the work place.[13] Art differentiates the beautiful from the ugly, the civilized from the primitive, art from kitsch, the subject from the nonsubject. For not only does artistic discourse fashion the representation of peoples, it also discriminates who is to be represented and who represents.[14]

These and other discourses designate alterity by denoting essential and characteristic distinctions, differentiae such as race, region, nationality, ethnicity, religion, and language, as well as those of class, time, age, and gender. These features are read as antithetical differentiae that prove the marginality that they designate. Tautologically, art confirms superior racial beauty and a higher degree of civilization; science, superior intelligence, and the transcending of superstition; religion and law, superior soul and body; history, the correct sequence of ascendance to that superiority. Historical discourse is especially significant in that the hegemonic history is the dominant narrative, the official version of reality to date as well as the plot for the future.

The rhetoric of monologic colonial discourse can be observed to proceed as follows. Subjectification of the other is realized by the rhetoric of antithesis and synecdoche. The centripetal forces of antithesis exteriorize the other. The colonial self is present, here and central, the other, there and marginal, absent. The self differs *in essence* from the other. *They* are not like *us:* they are not our color; their god is not God; their beliefs are not true, not science, and so on. Antithesis allows for an open troping by which the other can be relegated to anything beyond the borders of self: the other is colored, pagan, superstitious; the other is primitive, savage, beast.[15] The more intense the monologism, the more open the troping, the more extreme the alterity.

Within the range of potential antithetical tropes, synecdoche functions to locate the troping of the other within a narrow band of essential homogeneity. The rhetoric of antithesis restricts heterogeneity to the dominant self, and synecdoche acts to disallow individuation to the other. To know one is to know all. The characteristics of the group are the characteristics of each individual. Within acceptable and well-defined parameters, the others are all the same. And yet there is the occasional interstice in the homogeneity, when the rhetoric is forced to recognize an "individual" other: the good slave, the Indian scout, the token "spook who sat by the door." But the number of such individuals must be severely restricted in order to maintain the image of homogeneity, that image that ensures the verisimilitude of the antithesis.

Not only is subjectivity fashioned through, and are actions informed by, the rhetoric of the dominant discourse, but identity and action are legitimated through a strategy of ultimate referentiality. Colonial discourse aspires toward a system of representation in which word is linked contiguously with reality, in which hegemonic story is true history. For the aspiration of monologue is the aspiration for the single language, single voice, and single version of social relationships.[16] Monologic authority is vested in the metonymic organization of discursive elements into the correct combinations that constitute the true history and the real political borders. Colonial discourse emphasizes referent and content, appropriating the epistemes of "truth" and "reality" in an endeavor to surpass metonymy and achieve the status of mirror, where the word reflects exactly and uniquely the world. This is to say, the hegemony envisions so contiguous a discourse that the troping collapses from consciousness and the power of discursive representation is rewritten as the power of literal presentation. It eschews the chaotic relativities of dialogue and the substitution of metaphors and aims, instead, at apodeictic reference to the world.

This so referentially "true" discourse is not, however, aphasic discourse, as Jakobson would describe a solely metonymic discourse, but a *phasic* one that oscillates between the axis of combination (metonymy and synecdoche) and the axis of selection (metaphor and irony). The contents of the ethnocentric and racist trope can range from "cannibal" and "redskin" to "animal" and "noble savage." But the form of relating those tropes, the organizing strategy, is combinatory rather than selective, syntagmatic rather than paradigmatic, and metonymic rather than metaphoric. Alternate versions of social relationships, that is, alternate paradigms, are proscribed through the prohibition of dialogue. Instead, the monologue of the mirror presents the authorized versions of reality, truth, telos. Rhetoric is refashioned as logic, and tropes disappear in a semantics of reference in which the meaning of the other *is* the trope for the other. The monologue strings together discourses favorable for the physical domination of a people, from the writing of stereotypes, to the creation of slaves, to the making of genocide.

These "truths" shape the "reality" in which the relative presence and absence of the other is juggled. Antithetically, the other is generally rendered absent, exteriorized from the central and present self. But at times, the other is brought into dangerous proximity. During physically violent encounters, as in the conquest, the other is at once vividly represented as a dangerous presence and is effaced of full humanity. A present body, absent voice, absent humanity. Necessary for conquest, and for genocide, is the "truth" that the colonized is in some ways both dangerous and inferior, perhaps as wild beasts are. The other is a homogeneous menace, significant yet generalized, dangerous yet never humanly present.

In contexts of relatively diminished physical force, the other is more fully relegated to the realm of absence. The more fully realized the physical subjugation is, the less is the need to represent a dangerous proximity, and so the less the other need be envisioned present. Further, the other is denied discursive presence, both in the sense that the other is relatively absent from the vocabulary of the dominant discourse and in the sense that the other is absent as an agent of discourse. The other becomes nondiscursive and noninteractive, and approaches the status of text: static, extant, "true." The hegemony restricts access to active discourse to itself. The other is textualized, and according to traditional Western metaphysics, the written text, the literal other, is denied presence: the other is exteriorized, frozen, inscribed. Effectively, the other is silenced, existing only as defined by a rigid and prescribed alterity or not existing at all.

Chicanos are products of two colonial contexts. The first begins with the explorer Colón and the major event of the Renaissance: the "old" world's "discovery" of the "new." Spanish colonization of the Americas lasted more than three centuries, from the middle of Leonardo Da Vinci's lifetime to the beginning of Queen Victoria's. The first century is marked by conquest and true genocide: in Mexico alone, the indigenous population is cut down 96 percent, from 25 million to 1 million. The modern Mexican and Chicano descend from the miscegenation of Spaniard and Indian and the cultural encounter of conquistador and native. The second colonial context begins with the immigration of Austin's group from Connecticut to Texas, Mexico. Within one generation of Mexico's decolonization from Spain, two wars were waged in which Anglo America conquered Mexico and acquired its northern half. People were acquired with the lands, and the "Americanization" of natives in Texas, New Mexico, and California is analogous to that of natives in Manhattan, the Dakotas, Puerto Rico, or Hawaii. But because only half of Mexico was acquired, immigration can still figure largely in the constitution of the Chicano. Conversely, the territory of the Navajo, like that of the Puerto Rican, is entirely circumscribed by the United States; there can be only internal migration.[17]

Yet, for the Chicano, as for the Indian, the history of subjugation at home delimits the process of subject making. For both groups, alterity has coincided with the erasure of the other domain, the other space having been assimilated by the United States: Chicanos and Indians are rendered aliens from and in their own lands, internally colonized. The colonizer never left Indian nor Chicano space, neither Manhattan nor San Francisco. Shaping the original conception of the conquests, its subsequent rationalization, and its eventual erasure from U.S. consciousness, colonial discourse represented and continues to represent Chicanos and Indians as marginal and inferior others.

Both are not real Americans in many senses, including the linguistic, and for both "being" "American" remains problematic. To a large degree, both the colonial Indian and Chicano subjects are constructed according to the representation of their linguistic practices. The Indian, at the time of the conquest and when compared to the middle-class WASP archetype upheld as the American national self, is relatively less literate. Anglo America is both deaf and blind to Indian expression. This is read as "proof" of inferiority. Indigenous languages had no words for Jesus, for money, for opera;

ergo, the Indian is uncivilized, savage, and quite likely, subhuman.[18] And by extrapolation, Indians can only benefit from conquest: that is, it renders Indians civilized; genocide and colonialism save Indians' souls; and further, Indians are so worthless in their "wild" stage that the world would lose little at their elimination. Such is the rhetoric that forgets the complete extermination of some Indian people and the suppression of the rest.

A threshold marked by the ability to write separates Civilized Man from the savage beings; and among the literate, human worth is appraised, at least in part, according to the relative values ascribed in a hierarchy of languages. The Chicano subject may be subaltern, but insofar as, and to the degree that, the subject is Hispanic, the Chicano is human. And since Spanish is relatively close to English in the linguistic hierarchy, the suppression of Hispanic America is more problematic and of a different order than the nearly absolute suppression of Algonquian, Athapascan, or Uto-Aztecan America.[19] The presence of an alternative, extant, and *literate* linguistic tradition causes a crisis for Anglo America: not only does it preclude the status for English as sole, unchallenged mode for civilized American discourse, but it also undermines several myths that are at the very heart of the self-image propagated by Anglo America.

Part of the inspiration, orchestration, and rationalization for New World colonialism lies in the troping of the Americas as a new world and in the paramount role envisioned for the Anglo-American. Anglo-American mythology would have it that the United States is so much more than a mere extension of Western Europe, that it is the first blank slate since Eden, the new and perhaps last chance to get things right. Anglo-Americans met the challenge and performed that most elemental and significant of linguistic acts: the monologic, Adamic act of ascribing meaning, naming the new items in the new world. They inscribed themselves American Adams, invented new political institutions, forged new cities in the peopleless (not counting savages) wilderness.

History is a narrative, made story with plot, with telos, with heroes and villains. The United States locates itself at the climax and terminus of the trajectory of Western Civilization that began at the original

Eden. The move west, from Eden to the thirteen colonies, traces not only the spatial relocation but, more importantly, the historical development of civilization proper, through Greece and Rome, the English 're-'naissance, and peaking at the American naissance of Adam Jr. Egypt, the rest of Africa, and the "Orient," of course, are ignored. And according to Western cartography, the West does not stop at Appalachia; there is a manifest destiny; civilization was destined to move as far west as possible, to the edge of that ultimate boundary with the East, to that ultimate "shining sea."

And en route west, the Anglo encountered Indian and Chicano, both of whom left traces in the dominant discourse. Indian names and words have been taken to describe American places, athletic teams, motor homes. The use of these terms evokes pride in the conquest, much in the same manner as a mounted animal head does for the hunter. After all, the actual people, the Indians, have been successfully contained: first, their numbers have been thoroughly diminished; and second, those remaining are powerless, have the shortest life spans and highest infant mortality rates, and either are collected in remote areas far from Anglo-Americans or are somehow invisible in the cities. The conquest of the "wild west" has been so efficient, the containment of the "redskins" so thorough, that contemporary mention of these peoples is read by Anglo America as allusion to the cast of colorful characters in American history, beginning with Pocahontas and ending with Geronimo. On the national level, the Indian exists as story, not as living human. There can be no dialogue with the Indian text; the Indian can only be written about or read. The Indian is thoroughly contained and can no longer pose a menacing threat.[20] Because of this, the second Wounded Knee can become a cause célèbre, Dennis Banks and Russell Means become inscribed beside Sitting Bull: the attack on Anglo America is so marginal and so contained that it can be romanticized; contemporary Indian resistance is understood through the narratives of nostalgia. After all, what *real* damage can those absent, silent, noble savages, those ecologically correct, happy campers do?

But since the conquest of Mexican territory, there persists a stubborn linguistic trace that belies Anglo-American image production and that is more difficult to contain than by simple appropriation for the naming of motor homes. Consider a particularly significant self-image. Anglo-Americans epitomize their imperialist spirit in the cowboy: independent, powerful, free, implacable, and ever moving westward through the vast wilderness, fashioning America. And as such, the cowboy represents the quintessential American. That cowboys appear only after the U.S. acquisition of northern Mexico is no mere coincidence: could the cowboy have occurred in Georgia or in Vermont – or in Surrey, at that?

And yet, the paramount Anglo-American is thoroughly contaminated by a Mexican, a Hispanic, presence. Cowboy attire, tools, occupation, food, music, and most telling, his own lingo continually reveal this other origin. The very language that marks the cowboy has a Spanish accent. Consider the cowboy lexicon and its context of Spanish language and border discourse: arroyo/*arroyo;* bukeroo/*vaquero;* canyon/*cañon;* chaps/*chaparreras;* cinch/*cincho;* cowboy/*vaquero;* desperado/*desperado;* hoosegow/*juzgado;* lariat/*la reata;* loco/*loco;* lasso/*lazo;* mesquite/*mesquite;* mustang/*mestengo;* pinto/*pinto;* ranch/*rancho;* renegade/*renegado;* rodeo/*rodeo.* But by selectively reading the heteroglossia, the cowboy icon is figured a singularly American and new phenomenon: the cowboy and his lingo are conceived as U.S. originals; the Spanish, Mexican, Chicano etymology is erased.[21]

The linguistic trace also persists in place names. When Anglo-Americans finally acquired the western edge, California, they found existing cities already named: San Diego, Los Angeles, San José, San Francisco. The western "wilderness" had been already inscribed by Hispanics, much as the contemporary Chicano neighborhood is inscribed with barrio-identifying graffiti placas. The new Eden had been denied Adam Jr.; things were already named, and, worse yet, they had been *written* well before he and she arrived. Even California, the prize of the conquest and today's most populous state, especially California, undermines the myth: California was named in Spanish a century before the Anglo baptism of the United States, the first Thanksgiving.

The Chicano incarnates the Hispanic (that is, literate, European, human, antecedent) inscription of America and makes evident the Anglo-American rhetorical postscript. Unlike the Indian trace, the

Chicano's remains threatening. There are so many more Chicanos than Indians. Los Angeles, for example, has the largest urban concentrations of both Indians and Chicanos in the nation. It is not rural New Mexico where Indians and Chicanos remain far from the national consciousness. Los Angeles is home to perhaps 80,000 Indians and perhaps 1.4 million Chicanos and other Latinos. In 1990, the population of Chicanos/Latinos in California alone was greater than the population of any of forty-two other states. Within California, Chicanos equal the combined total of all other minorities; in ten years, white non-Hispanics will fall from the position of majority, a position they hold, partially at least, when compared to Indians and Chicanos, because of a superior life span. In twenty-five years, the largest ethnic group in California will be Chicanos/Hispanics. In reaction to such rapid change, Anglo-American rhetoric constructs a Chicano subject with minimal presence, with maximum absence. The growing discrepancy between rhetorical "truth" and existential fact works toward the impending "white shock" when Anglo-Americans realize all is not as it seems. Witness the "shock" of Anglo-Americans at the reaction of Los Angeles blacks to the acquittals of police in the beating of Rodney King, "white shock" at the intensity of black perceptions of a racist here and now.

In order to foster an image of an America born in the English language, it becomes necessary to propagate a story of contiguous and historical English precedence. Millennia of Native American presence is easily glossed over because Westerners read nothing of it. Hispanic America is more difficult to dismiss, but this is accomplished nevertheless. For example, history is written not chronologically but from East to West so that Spanish is encountered by the likes of Austin and Fremont during the Western expansion late in U.S. history; it appears *historically* after English. Spanish is made alien, an immigrant language, no more contiguously linked to America than is German or Chinese. There must be no Hispanization of Anglo America, neither in its history nor in its future. Even cowboy lingo must be envisioned to arise from an English-only monologue; it must not resemble an interlingual caló. These moves are advanced rhetorically and not logically. The history and contiguity of Spanish in the Southwest is denied in history books, popular culture, and through language laws.

A correlative of the displacement of Spanish is the illiteracy of the Chicano. Chicanos are depicted as nonwriting subjects who did not produce literature until taught English by Anglo-Americans.[22] This erasure of a linguistic and literary tradition enhances the marginalization of Spanish, both from Anglo America and from the Chicano writer, and moves the Chicano from the pole of civilized Western European culture toward the pole of the illiterate savage. There is no Hispanic history of the Southwest and, besides, caló is no real language at all. Linguistically then the Chicano speaks a language that has no real claim to the Southwest, speaks it poorly (it is not real Castilian), and, worst of all, does not write it. In effect, the Chicano is like the Indian.

And in fact this is so declared: the Chicano is inscribed "savage," marginalized from the Eurocentric appellation "Hispanic." The Chicano is de-hispanized and written as dark, uncivilized Indian. The Spaniard is romanticized and relegated to the historical past: conquistador, mission padre, and aristocratic Californio.[23] The historical link is broken because of racial difference (Caucasian versus hybrid mestizo), because of linguistic difference (Castilian versus Mexican Spanish and caló), and because of chronological difference (Spaniards of the past versus Chicanos of the present). The myth of Zorro contains the Spanish element in a safe, remote past; today's Chicano is descended not from Zorro and the other Spanish Californios but, at best, from their servants. In effect, the Chicano is located between Europe and indigenous America, marginalized from the Spaniard, moved partially toward the savage. Both Indian and Spaniard, the constitutive elements of the Chicano's mestizaje, are deferred to a safe past and removed from consideration in the making of contemporary America. Envisioned both as "historical" and small in number, they pose little threat to American consciousness, and can be romanticized and distantly acknowledged in Thanksgiving and Old California. But the number of Chicanos, the most rapidly increasing number, threatens the verisimilitude of the Anglo-American vision.

The Chicano is not equated with the Indian because to do so would ascribe to the Chicano the status of native. Because of the border and Mexico, the Chicano can be envisioned as foreigner, so that after rhetorical gymnastics, the Anglo immigrant can write the self as the undisputed original civilized human occupant. Therefore, the Chicano is not indigenous. Chicanos are foreign immigrants and illegal aliens. The INS and the Texas Rangers attest to that.[24] Present-day Chicanos are divorced spatially from Mexicans south of the border, temporally from the Californio, and racially from the Indian. Chicanos are divorced from the Southwest and read instead as an immigrant labor force. Not the noble and savage Indian nor the genteel Californio Spaniard, the Chicano is the pest, is the bracero who had the audacity to stay and have children in gangs and on welfare.

One more point, a historical one: in order to project a narrative of the apex of democracy, the history of the U.S. military conquest of northern Mexico is written as a simple financial transaction. That Anglo America is superior and preferable must be self-evident, so there could not have been objection. The Chicano could not have wanted to resist colonization, let alone actually have done so. Therefore, the conquest of Northern Mexico was not imperialism; it was a bloodless transfer of title of an unpopulated territory. History simultaneously maintains that the Mexicans from California to Texas, who weren't there in the first place, welcomed U.S. incorporation in a very poor Spanish but not in writing.

In these ways, and in many, many other ways, Anglo-American colonial discourse subjectifies and contains; it minimizes the presence of the Chicano other. A heterogeneous group is represented as a marginal homogeneity. The authoritative discourse constitutes the colonist mythology and codifies the hegemony.

Chicano literary production can be read as the response to such discursive activity. Chicano poetry has opted for hybridization, a linguistic mestizaje, incorporating the languages and discourses at play in America. It tends to reject the monologue of either autocolonial, assimilationist, English-only verse or the monologue of nationalist Spanish-only verse. Instead, it opts for a multiple tongue, multivoiced literature of the border. The hegemony of Anglo-American representation and subjectification is dialogized by a mestizaje of heteroglot texts that assert Chicano heterogeneity and American heteroglossia.

Such literature produces a subjectivity that opposes hegemonic subjectification: the alternate subjectification of the other challenges the authoritative subjectification of the dominant self, juxtaposing a literary representation with a literal representation. For it is in the realm of the literary that orders other than the literal can be first envisioned.[25] And this literary dialogism is characteristic of Chicano poetry.

Consider the poem, "Poema en tres idiomas y caló"[26] by José Antonio Burciaga. It plays among four languages and clearly works in an other tongue:

> Poema en tres idiomas y caló
>
> Españotli titlan Englishic,
> titlan náhuatl titlan Caló
> ¡Qué locotl!
> Mi mente spirals al mixtli,
> buti suave I feel cuatro lenguas in mi boca.
> Coltic sueños temostli
> Y siento una xóchitl brotar
> from four diferentes vidas.
>
> I yotl distictamentli recuerdotl
> cuandotl I yotl was a maya,
> cuandotl, I yotl was a gachupinchi,
> when Cortés se cogió a mi great tatarabuela,
> cuandotl andaba en Pachucatlán.
>
> I yotl recordotl el tonatiuh
> en mi boca cochi
> cihuatl, náhuatl
> teocalli, my mouth
> micca por el English
> e hiriendo mi español,
> ahora cojo ando en caló
> pero no hay pedo

porque todo se vale,
con o sin safos.

[Poem in Three Idioms and Caló

Spanish between English
between Nahuatl, between Caló.
How mad!
My mind spirals to the clouds
so smooth I feel four tongues in my mouth.
Twisted dreams fall
and I feel a flower bud
from four different lives.

I distinctly remember
when I was a Maya,
when I was a Spaniard,
when Cortez raped my great great grandmother
when I walked over the Southwest.

I remember the sun
in my mouth sleeps
woman, Nahuatl
temple my mouth,
killed by the English
and wounding my Spanish,
now I limp walk in fractured Spanish
But there is no problem
for everything is valid
with or without safeties.]

Beasts and Jagged Strokes of Color

Juan Felipe Herrera's "Literary Asylums" concludes with the line, "Outside beasts and jagged strokes of color blur."[1] This is the ultimate statement of a long poem which is divided into three sections, "Writing," "Reading," and "Being." As a final line, it engages and eludes, yet does address the trajectory of thought articulated across its three sections. In one sense, the line responds to the poem's general concerns about representation, perspective, and subjectivity. In another and more specific sense, the line creates ambiguity, makes unfinalized sense critical of the project of authoritative representation. "Literary Asylums" is a Chicano poem: it interanimates voices along the national boundary between the United States and Mexico. As such, it simultaneously considers and performs "writing, reading, and being" on the border, the site of a full complement of cultural conflict.

Border verse makes lines of poetry from the competing lines of discourse that crisscross the border zone. Here, the articulation of discourse puts into play an articulation of being at the interface of two national languages. "Literary Asylums" and other Chicano poems play in a poetics of hybridization that calls to mind the quotidian cultural politics of hybridization in the material space of the frontier. What is at play is the formation of a Chicano subject coming to be amid the competing discourses of nation. By poetics of hybridization I mean to convey a *dialogic* poetics.[2] Two nations are imagined in English and in Spanish and differentiate themselves at a common border, yet Chicano border space is a heteroglot interzone, a hybrid overlapping of the two. The material border and the discourse of nation contribute to a poetics in such a way that Chicano poetry advocates what a superficial reading of Bakhtin would lead us to think is an oxymoronic goal – a dialogic poetry. "Literary Asylums" is one such poem. But for now let me suspend explication of its last line and embark on a long detour through a consideration of meaning on the border.

Border Sense

Consider the border: in the imagining of nation, it is the infinitely thin line that truly differentiates the United States from Mexico.[3] The absolute certainty of its discrimination instills confidence in national definition, for it clearly marks the unequivocal edge of the nation. Its perceived thinness and keenness of edge are necessary for the predication of national subjectivity, which defines itself as naturally occurring inside its borders and not occurring outside. The national subject is conceived as an ideal, so that individual differences are suppressed in order to envision a national type embodying only essential characteristics. The U.S.–Mexican border is perceived as the thin line of demarcation and ultimate edge of respective world views that foster two nations. In their differing the two nations are similar, for both formulate a self in exclusion of what lies across the line. The thin borderline cleaves two national narratives, two national monologues of ideal and finalized selves. So while the United States and Mexico differ by virtue of the content of their narratives, their common use of the border analogously structures their narrative lines. U.S. American and Mexican understand clearly how the other is constituted, and each uses the other as absolute foil to define the self.

And because of this, neither national can adequately perceive the Chicano. The narratives of nation are finalizing monologues of self that suppress dialogue with others. To the degree that one *is* American or Mexican, one is deaf (*gluxoj*) to others whose structures of definition differ. The Chicano lives not so much beside a notional borderline as in material borderlands where discourse is not Manichaean but finely gradated. And because the thin and severe borderline is an essential component in the narrative of the nation, the notion of a broader zone, a borderlands, is incomprehensible, for to begin to conceive Chicano space is to begin to erase the nation. The national narrative is univocal and when confronted with Chicano hybridization, it is not only deaf to one language (English or Spanish), it is also deaf to the fusion of hybridization. It is as unequivocally deaf to another language as it is deaf to interlingual play.

National world views (*krugozory*) incorporate narratives, such as history, which may at times seem novelistic but which when yoked to the task of the nation effectively function monologically. Chicano poetry presents itself as lyric and music, less interested in narrating the history of the nation than in hybridizing actively. Its metaphors for poetry are song; for the border, a wound; for Chicanos ourselves, there is the irony of self as animal, derived from the extremely inaccurate representations we are given. The border zone affords space for mestizaje, racial hybridization, and for floricanto, poetic hybridization. The border zone is the site where the intercourses of sex and discourse play at the making of the Chicano body and the Chicano subject.

A river from the Gulf of Mexico to El Paso and a wire fence from El Paso to the Pacific forms a line that is imagined to prohibit the transgression of language. Border police patrol the line, stop speakers, and fix nationalities. Two nations cleave along its edge and configure themselves in languages they imagine to cleave there too. The United States and Mexico dream themselves in different languages and dream those languages as essential to the self as the land. English signifies American; Spanish signifies Mexican.[4] This is clearly the case; it is demonstrated at border crossings every day. As Mexican Nobel Laureate, Octavio Paz observes in the *Labyrinth of Solitude*, "We can all reach the point of knowing ourselves to be Mexicans. It is enough, for example, simply to cross the border" (12).

The ultimate authority to arbitrate at the borderline is fundamental to conceiving the nation. The more unyielding the line and the more absolutely it segregates, the better it is able to define the nation. A thin border is preferable to a thick one because narrowness renders its discrimination unequivocal. Broadness invites ambiguity and subjects difference to an unclear zone and to a gray scale. In addition, the absolute lack of breadth of the ideal borderline ensures that there can be no gray inhabitants, for there is literally no space in the purely imaginary construct. The logic of the thin border is the logic that fashions the ideal nation, national subject, and national narrative. Border links to narrative through history, for the border is a historical line. It outlines, for example, the flow of U.S. imperialism, the ultimate extent of manifest destiny, and the ebb of Mexican territory after the U.S. conquest. And the logic of the thin border is applicable to history, where a narrow, unequivocal historical line is seen as most clearly narrating the nation. Like the border, the line of history defines the nations. As Paz observes, "To become aware of our history is to become aware of our singularity" (10). The logic of the thick border, however, is quite different.[5] As Gloria Anzaldúa observes in *Borderlands/La Frontera,* "A borderland is a vague and undetermined place created by the emotional residue of an unnatural boundary. . . . It is in a constant state of transition" (3).

The inhabitants of the border zone who partake in messy cultural interplay cannot be contained on the narrow conceptual axis of monologic nationalism. Their physical presence belies the fantastically thin border; they blur the hard-edged distinctions. They are ill defining and ill defined, and cannot become subjects in the same way as nationalists.[6] They cannot because for them there is no metonymic link of nation, place, language, and identity. The tendency to monologize is the driving force of identification for those who imagine possessing one land, one language, one history, and one national narrative. But this is not the case for those rendered aliens in their own lands or aliens in other lands. For in the zone of repeated culture clash, it is unmitigated homogeneity that remains illusory. The thin border marks the thick border's inhabitants a species apart, because, as Anzaldúa states, "Borders are set up to define the places that are safe and unsafe, to distinguish *us* from *them.* . . . The prohibited and forbidden are its inhabitants" (3).

The material border has a significant impact on the linguistic performance of the Chicano. Linguistic media contest at each articulation, always signifying something in terms of national alignment. Chicanos speak English. Chicanos speak Spanish. The majority do some degree of language mixing, some type of hybridizing.[7] Some primarily speak the hybridized argot, Chicano caló. In each case, the choice of language, in its effect on subject formation, can be neither disinterested nor indifferent. Linguistic articulation is read as national articulation by those imagining clear national difference. And in the borderlands there is always the bilingual backdrop of English and Spanish at the same time. The Chicano utterance plays against that backdrop, interanimating bordered differences in the act. This is perhaps why interlingual play is so prevalent in Chicano poetry: it is valorized in a poetics of hybridization that foregrounds in verse the discursive interplay of quotidian speech. And in a sense, this speaking style defines the Chicano: intercultural heteroglot.[8] To *be* Chicano is to negotiate difference; it is a process, an active interanimating of competing discourses. Chicano caló and hybridized poetics put into motion unfinalized selves, failing at monologue, falling outside national subjectivity. Dialogism makes for a continual coming to be.

Borderline Deaf

Perhaps the most concentrated narration of the Mexican character is to be found in Octavio Paz's *Labyrinth of Solitude*.[9] Paz begins his project of defining Mexicanness with a look to the edges: to the border and to Chicanos. In the first essay, "Pachuco and Other Extremes," Paz declares that the Mexican can know himself simply by crossing the border; for Paz, the border is a thin one and across it "Even the birds speak English" (18). The North American character reveals itself to him because across the shared border every characteristic illuminates recognition of difference in himself. That is simple. What is difficult for Paz is to consider a thick border. The Chicano remains elusive for him because the narration of the nation is blind to the borderlands and deaf to the voices there.

"Pachuco and Other Extremes" considers Los Angeles, the city with the most Mexicans (and/or Chicanos) after Mexico City. Its character, however, eludes Paz; he is surprised by "the city's vaguely Mexican atmosphere, which cannot be captured in words or concepts. This Mexicanism . . . floats in the air . . . 'floats' because it never mixes or unites with the other world, the North American world" (13). There is something barely tangible in the city, something that resists both alignment with the North American and comprehension by the Mexican. Paz finds a more disturbing ambiguity evident in the Los Angeles Chicano youth. "When you talk with them, you observe that their sensibilities are like a pendulum, but a pendulum that has lost its reason and swings violently and erratically back and forth. This spiritual condition, or lack of a spirit, has given birth to a type known as the *pachuco*" (13).[10]

The pachuco is a borderland inhabitant. What Paz considers a "lack of spirit" could well be the borderland condition to which his nationalist perspective has rendered him deaf. It is clear that Paz considers vacillation in regard to the nation wrong:

> The *pachuco* does not want to become a Mexican again; at the same time he does not want to blend into the life of North America. His whole being is sheer negative impulse, a tangle of contradictions, an enigma. Even his very name is enigmatic: *pachuco,* a word of uncertain derivation, saying nothing and saying everything. It is a strange word with no definite meaning; or, to be more exact, it is charged like all popular creations with a diversity of meanings. (14)

Paz's abhorrence of the lack of definite meaning or of the diversity of meanings reflects a monologic perspective, a perspective that by definition suppresses hybridity. So while "Everyone agrees in finding something hybrid about him, something disturbing and fascinating," Paz nevertheless finds the pachuco "a pariah, a man who belongs nowhere" (16, 17). The pachuco commits the sin of hybridization and of not affirming a national narrative.

> He denies both the society from which he originated and that of North America. When he thrusts himself outward, it is not to unite with what surrounds him but rather to defy it. This is a suicidal gesture, because the *pachuco* does not affirm or defend anything except his exasperated will-not-to-be . . . he is revealing an ulcer, exhibiting a wound. A wound that is also a grotesque, capricious, barbaric adornment. (17)

Suicide and the "exasperated will-not-to-be" are what the nationalist perspective sees of the impulse to hybridize. The pachuco's discourse is ineffectual because "his hybrid language and behavior reflect a physic oscillation between two irreducible worlds – the North American and the Mexican – which he vainly hopes to reconcile and conquer. He does not want to become either a Mexican or a Yankee" (18). The pachuco and the Chicano are enigmatic for Paz, but only as an aberration that can be ignored. For by crossing the thin border, Paz was able to define the nation: "We can all reach the point of knowing ourselves to be Mexicans. It is enough, for example, simply to cross the border" (12).

Alurista, the Chicano poet from Tijuana and San Diego, responds to this in the poem "Pachuco Paz":[11]

> we can all reach the point
> > of knowing ourselves
> > to be Mexicans in the north
> Mexican air with placas on walls   [graffiti]
> > names to be found
> or carvings be read
> > leaving no tracks
> or marcas in the wind   [marks]
> music is born
> > and la fiesta del silencio   [the festival of silence]
> permeates our hearts
> and our blood pounds a beat
> > to reach the point
> where and when, rhythmically
> > we know ourselves
> to be
> > chicanos de colorada piel   [Chicanos with red skin]
> > de espíritu guerrero   [with warrior spirit]
> hunting in our own land
> > nuestra tierra   [our land]

Alurista first responds to "Pachuco and Other Extremes" by playing with the Mexican author's name: Alurista takes *Paz* literally and offers a reading of "Pachuco Paz" as pachuco *peace.* The effect is to destabilize the Mexican's identity by focusing on name as a discursive act that is open to interpretation. And that interpretation is ironic, running contrary to the literal *peace,* for Paz attacks the pachuco with wounds, suicide, and a name that says nothing. Alurista's "Pachuco Paz" is double-voiced, first in the irony of Paz's meaning, and then in the literal definition that infuses Paz's name, that is, his self-definition.[12] The Chicano play with name-as-discourse is an act of dialogism; Alurista makes poetry of the refraction that breaks up the possibility of monologic vision. In effect, he recasts the Mexican's trip to Los Angeles from a trip across the borderline to a move into the borderlands.

"Pachuco Paz" works in its movement between two points, two chronotopes where subjectivity is worked out. The first is Alurista's appropriation of Paz's simple formula for self-knowledge, "We can all reach the point of knowing ourselves to be Mexicans. It is enough, for example, simply to cross the border." The first eight lines of the poem point to the inability of the Mexican to read the Chicano. For in the Mexican national vision, placas (neighborhood-specific graffiti) remain indecipherable, Chicano thought "floats" like an "atmosphere, which cannot be captured in words or concepts."[13] The second point begins at line nine, where Paz's inability to perceive Chicano texts visually is complicated by the delineation of oral and aural texts. Not only can the Mexican neither see nor read Chicano words, but his conception of writing is inappropriate for approaching Chicano texts. The Chicano poem is music, rhythm, and heartbeat, a festival of silence for those deaf to border discourse. The points contrast clearly: for Paz, self-definition occurs in the instant of border transgression, while for Alurista the where and when of selves happens in rhythm. For the Chicano there is no single flash of self-knowing, subjectivity is drawn out as in a musical performance. The nation eludes the Chicano who remains "hunting in our own land / nuestra tierra."

Alurista's poetry puts into play the poetics of hybridization. "Pachuco Paz" juggles national languages and discourses in order to juggle Chicano space in the borderlands. It takes up its position through various relations with the ambient discursive hierarchies. That this occurs in poetry is ironic, given Bakhtin's understanding of the poetic tendency to monologize. The tendency of verse toward monologism, toward the codification and finalization of national identity, this *epic* tendency is confronted by the borderland propensity for dialogism. In the Chicano context, for some reason, a dialogic poetry prevails and it is the narrative of nation that is perceived to be monologic. From the borderland perspective, the narrative of nation is not novelistic, that is, it is not like Bakhtin's notion of the novel, unfinalized and temporally oriented from the present toward an open future. Here, the narrative of nation is perceived in its capacity as authoritative line, as history (narrow line from past to present nation), as dead word blocks for the building of nation.

Alurista emphasizes the form of the form, that is, he focuses on hybridization itself. The reader of his poetry must actively negotiate interlingual terrain, often ultimately having to *write* in order to read. Chicano poetry is active, or perhaps interactive, because meaning is always coming to be in a dialogue between author and reader. In "Pachuco Paz," for example, the reader must choose how to read *Paz*. The poetics of hybridization opposes finalization in principle, and the Chicano realization of that poetics opposes the finalization of national identity through practice, since finalization terminates dialogue, and dialogue, for whatever reason, is the dominant Chicano discursive relation to the world. Because of this, the active coming to be of Chicanos is played out in the poem: unfinalized, hybridized, dialogic.

The tendency to read the Chicano dialogically opens the door to a broad range of readings. French philosopher Jean-Luc Nancy considers racial hybridization in terms of discursive dialogism. In "Cut Throat Sun," he ponders the Chicano's mestizaje, that is, miscegenation from European and Native American sources.[14] For Nancy the hybridization of race, like that of language, affects the Chicano notion of self. Mestizaje is a biological borderlands where bodies come to be in the competition among genetic codes. But Nancy is interested not in race as essence but in mestizaje as process. He views the mestizo as unfinalized subject and as such, difficult to discuss. "Reservation: Isn't it already going too far to talk about *mestizaje?* As if *mestizaje* were 'some thing,' a substance, an object, an identity (an identity!) that could be grasped and 'processed.'" What Nancy contributes to the consideration of the Chicano/pachuco/mestizo is the temporal expansion of the borderland chronotope. While others increase the width of the border to a material space for the living, Nancy increases the aspect of time. "*Mestizaje* is always a very long, vast and obscure story. It is such a slow process that no one can see it happening. A single *mestizo* does not make for *mestizaje*. It takes generations – and more, an imperceptible drift towards infinity" (122). The unfinalizability of the mestizo stems not only from hybridity but from the extreme length of time that the process of mestizaje takes. The nonmestizo, the imagined racial purebred, is finalized because there are no factors contributing to its coming to be. While the purebred exists self-referentially, the mestizo is still making sense.[15] "A *mestizo* is someone who is on the border, on the very border of *meaning*." The mestizo is unfinalized and its meaning is not frozen because it is still becoming. In this sense, one cannot *be* a mestizo. From this perspective, when Mexico identifies itself as a nation of mestizos, it finalizes mestizaje in creating the national subject: Mexican but no longer mestizo. The Chicano too, in identifying the self as mestizo racial subject or as Chicano national subject, finalizes it.

The Chicana border philosopher, Gloria Anzaldúa, provides a metaphor that recalls Paz and Alurista to the living border. In "The Homeland, Aztlán/El otro México," the opening chapter of *Borderlands/La Frontera*, Anzaldúa states: "The U.S.-Mexican border *es una herida abierta* where the Third World grates against the first and bleeds. And before a scab forms it hemorrhages again, the lifeblood of two worlds merging to form a third country – a border culture" (3). The border is an open wound bleeding between two nations. A third country (though not nation) and a border culture emerges in the active bleeding and the confluence of bloods. In short, the borderlands are the site for ongoing hybridization, where being occurs in the blood flow before it can be fixed in a scab.[16] Anzaldúa's metaphor of the border-as-wound recalls Paz's vision of the pachuco's wound as "grotesque, capricious, barbaric adornment." In their own ways, both Anzaldúa and Paz view the Chicano as flaunting the border. This flaunting is the rejection of nation for Alurista, who in his introduction to *Nationchild Plumaroja* again responds to Paz, "we do not recognize capricious borders on the Red Continent."[17]

Borderland Singing

Lorna Dee Cervantes also addresses the border lesion in verse: "Let me show you my wounds: my stumbling mind, my / 'excuse me' tongue, and this / nagging preoccupation / with the feeling of not being good enough."[18]

Cervantes's poems often work out the relationship of writing and coming to be in the borderlands. Her first book, *Emplumada,* and the forthcoming *Bird Ave* locate the poems' enunciation in San José, California, her hometown and the Chicano center of Northern California. The poems chart the transgressing lines and contending trajectories that cross her home, often in the metaphor of border-crossing, migratory birds. The titles of her collections tell of her use of that metaphor; both emerge from the vocabulary of birds. The Spanish title orchestrates a range of tropes that color the text: *Emplumada,* that is, pen, feather, pen flourish, plumage. *Bird Ave,* on the other hand, functions as the straightforward street address, Bird Avenue, but also as ambiguous, interlingual play: Bird *ave,* that is, Bird *bird.* Both titles point to the central metaphor of birds and their migratory crossings, and further, both assert an interlingual dynamic of English and Spanish in dialogue.

While the migratory bird metaphor addresses the multiple transgressions of the borderline, it is the interlingual play that actually enacts the poetics of hybridization of the border zone. Cervantes's poems play out such a poetics in their repeated pitting of discourse against discourse. Hers is a polyphonic poetry set in the material space of San José, a heteroglot poetry in which discourse engages alternative discourse. Her home is a site of hybridization where any articulation is infused with, marked by, discursive alterity. The lines of contention do not simply cross, but rather lacerate and pull apart the border space.

It is worth noting that her second collection of poetry abandons the bird metaphor for the virulent title, *From the Cables of Genocide*.[19]

An examination of *Emplumada* reveals Cervantes's employment of the poetics of hybridization. Border transgression, north and south crossing, is the subject of two poems, "Oaxaca, 1974" and "Visions of Mexico While at a Writing Symposium in Port Townsend, Washington." South is not only to Mexico but further to Mexico's South, to the Native (and largely non-Spanish speaking) city of Oaxaca. "Oaxaca, 1974" enacts in interlingual dialogue the deafness of Mexico to the migrant Chicana, the inability of Mexican nationals to engage Chicano speech. While "My brown body searches the streets / for the dye that will color my thoughts," "México gags, / Esputa! / on this bland pochaseed."[20] In Mexico, Chicano discourse is only read as defect, a negation, with pocha signifying a weak, faded, lacking Mexican.

"Visions of Mexico" first moves south to Mexico, then north. In the section "México" communication is nonverbal: "When I'm that far south, the old words / molt off my skin," "I watch and understand," "We work / and watch seabirds elbow their wings / in migratory ways, those mispronouncing gulls / coming south / to refuge or gameland." Chicano discourse is represented in a manner reminiscent of Alurista's music, rhythm, and heartbeat: for Cervantes it is music, rhythm, heartbeat, and animal:[21]

> My sense of this land can only ripple through my veins
> like the chant of an epic corrido.
> I come from a long line of eloquent illiterates
> whose history reveals what words don't say.
> Our anger is our way of speaking,
> the gesture is an utterance more pure than word.
> We are not animals
> but our senses are keen and our reflexes,
> accurate punctuation.
> All the knifings in a single night, low-voiced
> scufflings, sirens, gunnings . . .
> We hear them
> and the poet within us bays.

"Visions of Mexico" moves north in the section "Washington," and significantly, North is not simply north of the national borderline, but north of the borderlands. In Washington, the Chicana again confronts a monologic world view: in the North, Chicanos are envisioned in stereotypes or not at all. "I heard them say: México is a stumbling comedy. / A loose-legged Cantinflas woman / acting with Pancho Villa drunkenness. / Last night at the tavern / this was all confirmed / in a painting of a woman." Yet the purpose of the trek north is to gain writing skills, skills that when employed by the Chicana can express the ineffable and belie the stereotypes.

> there are songs in my head I could sing you
> songs that could drone away
> all the Mariachi bands you thought you ever heard
> songs that could tell you what I know
> or have learned from my people
> but for that I need words
> simple black nymphs between white sheets of paper
> obedient words   obligatory words   words I steal
> in the dark when no one can hear me
>
> as pain sends seabirds south from the cold
> I come north
> to gather my feathers
> for quills

Several of the poems wage the intercultural warfare of California on the pages of *Emplumada*. "Poema Para Los Californios Muertos" is a particularly potent criticism of the use of history on the border. The poem reacts in rage to a historical plaque that makes token reference to the Mexican inhabitants of preconquest California. "Yo recuerdo los antepasados muertos. / Los recuerdo en la sangre, / la sangre fértil" [I remember the dead ancestors. I remember them in my blood, my fertile blood]. "In this place I see nothing but strangers. / On the shelves there are bitter antiques, / yanqui remnants / y estos no de los Californios" [Yankee remnants and those not of the Californios].

The strongest condemnation of the deafness of others to the borderlands is "Poem for the Young White Man Who Asked Me How I, an Intelligent, Well-Read Person Could Believe in the War Between Races." After delineating a utopia of poetry and peace, "Poem for the Young White Man" describes a violent borderland where racial warfare abounds, where the poet/speaker is attacked. "I'm marked by the color of my skin. / The bullets are discrete and designed to kill slowly. / They are aiming at my children. / These are facts." "Every day I am deluged with reminders / that this is not / my land / and this is my land." In describing a situation unimaginable to the young white man, the poet acknowledges that their different world views are in conflict. Cervantes undermines the "truth" of the other's views, yet simultaneously undermines and advances her own. "I believe in revolution / because everywhere the crosses are burning, / sharp-shooting goose-steppers round every corner, / there are snipers in the schools . . . / (I know you don't believe this, / You think this is nothing / but faddish exaggeration. But they / are not shooting at you.)" The words "these are facts" and "you think this is nothing but faddish exaggeration" accomplish several things. First, they establish the veracity of the speaker and undercut the authority of the young man's objection. But in addition, when read after the hyperbole of "sharp-shooting goose-steppers round every corner," the objecting claim to "exaggeration" seems warranted. In other words, the poem has it ambiguously both ways. In Cervantes's hybridized poetics, *truth* is not possible if one participant in dialogue is deaf; truth is constructed among the hearing and speaking participants. In California, truth is dialogic.

It is no wonder then that in the homeland of *Emplumada,* where the Mexican and the Anglo-American are deaf to Chicano hybrid discourse, Chicano identity itself is extremely problematic. In "Barco de Refugiados," for example, Chicanos are denied the thin borderline that has been crossed by so many other immigrants, from Puritan refugees at Plymouth Rock to Vietnamese refugees in Silicon Valley. That hard-edged separator of nations is drawn out for Chicanos, who are therefore never permitted to transgress cleanly, clearly. For Chicanos the refugee ship is "El barco que nunca atraca" [The ship that will never dock]. And yet, as borderland inhabitants, we are afforded a keen sense of hearing. In "From Where We Sit: Corpus Christi" those of us who read hybrid verse can hear and understand those whom tourists, those international border crossers, cannot. We are not deaf to the language of birds:

> We watch seabirds flock the tour boat.
> They feed from the tourist hand.
>
> We who have learned the language
> they speak as they beg
>
> understand what they really say
> as they lower and bite.

The tourist, the Mexican, and the young white man are deaf to Chicano discourse; they can hear something but it must sound like the inarticulate growl and coo of beasts.

"Outside Beasts and Jagged Strokes of Color Blur"

Let us now return to the last line of "Literary Asylums" and conclude our detour through the border. Juan Felipe Herrera ends "Literary Asylums" in bright light; he is concerned with the quality of vision, with the sharply focused and with the blur. The poem extends through "Writing," "Reading," and "Being" and articulates a discourse of class. The borderland inhabitant is not merely Chicano, pachuco, and mestizo, but the "unrich" as well. And to the realm of the deaf, the Mexican, the tourist, the white man, Herrera appends the blind, the artist. Artistic representation is offered as metaphor for discursive relationships.

In "Writing," the first section, *true* writing and history are presented as the expression of the power of the rich. The rich view the work of the unrich as "verses from the colony of beasts." The rich observe that the unrich "beast obeys the master's wish" but wonder if given authority, "Will they still obey an invisible voice? Will the creatures be able to pronounce / the new language? / What words? What signs? What writing?" The vision of the poor as beasts seems clearly ironic, but in "Writing," the beast-like character of the unrich is confirmed in ambiguous lines, "Obviously, unrich writers are not animals, not reptiles. It does not matter / They are prowling at the master's gate." In "Reading," the unrich reader and listener is described as "the conquered, the unkempt, the wounded, the forgotten . . . ," terms that recall Paz's description of the pachuco as the pariah with a wound.

Who is a beast and who has the authority to so call one? This is what is at stake in "Literary Asylums." The poetics of hybridization asserts that "truth" and meaning are worked out in dialogue, but what sort of dialogue is possible with the visual representation of the blind yet powerful? And even if one can paint another as a beast, what does it mean? This is answered in the last line, albeit ambiguously so.

In considering "Outside beasts and jagged strokes of color blur," it seems that particular significance rests in the last word, "blur." But in working toward it linearly, we are first confronted with *outside*. *Outside* is not *inside* and so is differentiated by a thin but absolute line. It is not so much another *inside* as it is the absence of *inside*. It is some zone beyond the margins of civilized humanity, the territory of marginalized human *beasts*. "Jagged strokes" either cut or paint *color*, that is, race or hue. If we posit "jagged strokes of color" as metonym for visual representation and metaphor for writing, then we enable at least two readings of the *blur*, the inside and the outside readings.

The meaning of the last line from the inside perspective might be paraphrased as "The poor and their depiction by the rich meld and cannot be differentiated" or, again, "The images of the poor held by the rich are true." Here the act of blurring reinforces authoritative representation: signifier and signified collapse into an existential essence, what is said, *is*. Such blurring underscores the belief in a harmonious correspondence between *inside story* and *outside reality*. It asserts the absolute accuracy of *inside* representation and obscures any question of turning the gaze back upon the project of *inside* writing or upon the slant of *inside* stories. The logic of this blurring is the logic of the thin border, for it rests upon the absolute distinction between *inside* and *outside*, a logic by which the blurring of others sharpens the view of self. It may seem ironic that the sharp-edged border between the two is supported by blurry vision; but in that the logic of the thin border is monologic, this makes sense. For the monologic differentiation of self and other prohibits dialogue that would work toward dialogic truths. Monologic *truth* is deaf and nearly blind. It can therefore imagine others as beasts. The blurred images of beasts and the fuzzy hearing of growls and coos is the work of the single line.

A reading from the *outside,* however, could be quite different. "Outside beasts and jagged strokes of color blur" could be read from the borderlands as "The poor and their self-depiction distort representation by the rich" or "The self-image of the poor belies the image held by the rich." From the *outside,* blurring impugns the melding of signifier with signified and its consequent corroboration of the "inside" world view, and instead obscures that vision. It is a parallax view that undermines the absolute authority of any monocular perspective. Consideration of perspectival and contextual difference weakens *inside* claims for authority because it opens the possibility for dialogue. From the borderlands perspective, blurring dialogizes.

There are, of course, more ways to read that one line of verse. But to consider other meanings for *blur* is to enter dangerous territory, where poets bay and a vague Mexicanism floats in the air. And there on the border of meaning, one might lose oneself.

Space and Time

Small Sea of Europe

At the end of the eighteenth century, Hindu law, insofar as it can be described as a unitary system, operated in terms of four texts that "staged" a four-part episteme defined by the subject's use of memory: *sruti* (the heard), *smriti* (the remembered), *sastra* (the learned-from-another), and *vyavahara* (the performed-in-exchange).

– Gayatri Chakravorty Spivak

In Europe's small sea,
a system of exchange:
forms of life
and motion in sign.

The Case In Point –

Verkehr:
'the motion of women, of slaves,
in sleekcongested automobiles, trunks
with drugs'

Verkehr,
from the Sanscrit (small sea),
vyavahara:
'performance traffic,
former act of transformation,
an exchange.'

Ecos escritos: *Sruti, Smriti, Sastra*
three sisters in myth, very
sources of Europe, Western Man,
the very sounds slipping: 3Ss, sans(é)crit
3Ss:
3Ss: ecos escritos (S grito)

Again, then.
Verkehr:
S₁ in the automobile beside S₂, S₃
at the wheel, 'Sister . . .' furtive, slave-like
movements (escape? from/to what/where?)
But who can drive? Of course, S₂ remembers,
tells, S₁ hears, inserts the key,
demonstrates, S₃ learns, starts the motor: of
course, escape, With-Drugs o wild & steering slave
through furtive traffic, changing lanes, exchanging
places of courses, escape:
Sruti hears, Smriti recalls, Sastra learns from an other:
S drive and drive, verkehr
S *verkehr:* vyavahara
a performance, vyavahara,
the S sound of abandon.

(Or) Again:
Sastra (née 'furtive slave') learned
furtive from
Sruti: (née 'furtive slave') heard
furtive from
Smriti (née 'furtive slave') remembers
furtive from
the small sea of history, the big C of capital,
first squirt of legend, transcendental quill
and myth-inks, rib stain here first
no ear, no hearing, across which sheets first
defined smear.
I remember Smriti, in the dictionary,

Verkehr:
'fast women in cars escape with drugs'
like Texas, but this is Berlin
to Paris, night rides hard riding off course
3 woman Ss written off across this old sad continent
fast esses, stained-fast essences, the Ss senses (S sense)
of woman defi(l/n)ed.
Some big *Dichtung*
this place,
a ce.

— London, 1988

Blood Points

Beginning

Women taught me to read from left to right. Women taught me the order of the alphabet and the sequence of numbers. They taught me that in the beginning the word was made flesh. At home, at school, and at catechism, it was women who first taught me the order of the universe. I learned grammar, syntax, and history; order, class, and phylum; and I learned to write cursive, pushing and curving ever to the right.

Sense, I was taught, lay at the end of the sentence. To find it I had to attend to the subject, verb, and object of syntax as well as to the past, present, and future of tense. This was taught to me as a plan for life. To get to the sense of anything, I had to read it, and to read it, I had to follow the rules. The basic rule was simple: begin at the beginning and end at the end. Finding sense was the same as finding a place, and the process of understanding was the same as physically moving from origin to destination. This made the reading of maps especially rewarding, for there sense and place were one. I had been taught to value the continuous and the contiguous, to appreciate the next event in the novel, the next rest stop on the highway. One point leads to the next, and if I attended to their proper order, I would reach my desired ends.

This point by point order provided the underlying structure for apprehending the world. A thing gained meaning because of its location in relation to the *where* and *when* of other things. Sense was predicated upon where something was in space, when it was in time, and what was around it. The order of spatial relationships is that of contiguity, so that to be beside or south means something quite different than to be far away or north. If something is desired, presence is better than absence: it is better that the loved one, for example, is beside you rather than in San Bernardino. Proximity has meaning for us, for without it, how else could sense be made of a saying such as "poor Mexico, so far from god and so close to the United States"? The order of temporal relationships is that of continuity, so that now or always means something different than past or never. The enumeration of time is especially fortuitous in this regard, for it facilitates the placing of events in proper sequence. That the United States took California from Mexico in 1848 and that gold was discovered there in 1848 means something. And if we factor in place, it is clear that it means something different south of the border than it does north. And so I follow the line, in space and in time, apprehending the world.

Part One

In the small world of a book, I am faced with stories by women that I want to read. The thin yellow volume of *Cuentos Chicanos* is filled with an ascending sequence of contiguous pages.[1] Next to each other, one after the next, lie two stories, "Ghost Talk" by Ana Castillo and "Willow Game" by Denise Chávez. "Ghost Talk" begins on page 48 and continues to page 55; "Willow Game," from 56 to 63. "Ghost Talk" begins with the demonstrative pronoun *this,* and "Willow Game" ends with punctuation, an ellipsis. Between *this* and the ellipsis, two stories proceed. I come prepared to read and to get to the meaning of the stories in the way I have been taught. I begin at the beginning, ready to follow the narration of events from the first to the last. I read confident that the proper order of events can only proceed, like time and like cause and effect, irreversibly one way, to one end. But neither "Ghost Talk" nor "Willow Game" follows the rules. They seem to narrate little and instead rely heavily on some other order. What narrative there is seems there to introduce violence, so that it is as if narrative itself comes to signify violence.

First "Ghost Talk." I read "Ghost Talk" from beginning to end, but right away there is a problem. It begins with the same words with which it ends: "This is the city where it all happened/happens. The one movie directors love so much." At first this seems that, rather than progressing from A to Z, it goes from A back to A. But this is actually not so difficult: as long as the intermediary points follow in sequence, it is possible to imagine a journey that ends where it began. This can be imagined for a journey around the world as well as for a journey through a short story. That could explain the "happened/happens" too: what occurred in the past at the beginning occurs again in the present at the end.

But there is more. "Ghost Talk" does not really tell a story until the second half. It does not narrate events in a chronological sequence in the beginning but does something quite different. The first half of "Ghost Talk" follows the eye as it moves from point to point in the city, describing one thing, then moving to the next. Time is confused because there is no apparent flow and because there is a retrospect from memory. The reading from beginning to end follows some sort of order, an order that is perhaps described as a spilling from one sentence over to the next:

> i catch a glimpse of her profile in a store window. Her hair is cut shoulder length, the Indian braid buried somewhere in a bureau drawer. It is the cut of a woman well on her way to conservative middle age, some days it is lustrous and sexy. You have sexy hair, the hair stylist says, running a comb lovingly through it, then corrects herself as if women are not supposed to say such things to women. My mother said i looked like Greta Garbo and Juana said i should be in an Italian movie. (48)

"Ghost Talk" spills forward this way, sentence by sentence, guided by the eye from city site to sight, by the mind through memory, and narrated by the "i" through a synecdoche of the body, in the "cut of a woman."

But then just past half way, the style changes abruptly and a sequential narrative ensues. At this point, on page 52, the story begins to make sense. The narrator tracks down her absent father with the intention to kill. The narrative sequence begins with attention to the body, to its parts, to its origin:

i don't have a square back like Indians do, and my legs are curved, not birdlike. But i think people don't get past that. They focus on the narrow eyes, dark skin, the full lips and black straight hair. i don't tell anybody my father was white. (52)

The narrator is the daughter of a Mexican mother and a white father. We learn that he ignored her and mistreated her mother. She confronts him with a gun, but he falls victim to a heart attack. The sequence of events is easy to follow. It is a story of an avenging mestiza. It is about race, gender, and generation politics.

But that "Ghost Talk" ends where it began, that so much of the story is imagistic, that it simultaneously happened/happens leaves me confused and denies me the ordered comfort I expect to derive from a narrative. In order to make sense of it as a whole, it is necessary, I think, to pay special attention to the transitional paragraph. "Ghost Talk" shifts to narrative in a moment of self-reflection, when parts of the body and the origin of the body are considered. Reflection on the mestiza body forces a look back in time, a reflection that looks at the body as the effect of an original cause, miscegenation. The story of mestizaje begins with the violent act of the white father, and "Ghost Talk" ends with violence directed at him. And in this, the narrative at the end of "Ghost Talk" provides the ultimate point for the whole of it. The story ends after the desire to know the body, its parts and origin, that is, it ends after the desire to narrate the body. The ultimate sense of it, after all, lies in the knot in which narrative, body, and violence are bound. The story of the mestiza body is the sequence of blood in the site of blood.

Immediately after "Ghost Talk" there comes "Willow Game." Compared to "Ghost Talk," "Willow Game" seems much more the traditional story. However, it also ends with a narrative twist (in this case, there are actually two), which ultimately shapes the meaning of the story. But what is striking about "Willow Game" is how it moves from point to point. In the order of the narration, the temporal is subordinate to the spatial. Over and over, points are made because of some relation in space.

The story is essentially the coming of age of a young girl. It is told in events, but more importantly, it is related on a neighborhood grid, a triangle marked by three trees: "Our house was situated in the middle of the block and faced outward to a triangle of trees that became both backdrop and pivot of this child's tale" (57). Meaning accrues because of proximity to the Apricot tree, the Marking-Off tree, the Willow tree. Consider the description of the Marking-Off tree:

> The tree was a reference point, offering no shade, but always mediation. It delineated the Up world from the Down. It marked off the nearest point to home, without being home; it was a landmark, and as such, occupied our thought, not in the way the Apricot tree did, but in a subtler, more profound way. (58–9)

The story continues this way, meaning is delineated across space, between points. In the plan of the narrator's life, the Willow tree occupies a prime position. "There to our left is the Willow tree, completing this trinity of trees. How to introduce you to her?" (59).

Certain events in the narrator's life originate outside the home in the house next door. When the Cardozas lived there, it was the "senseless boys, demon boys": Mannie who "punched the hole in our plastic swimming pool" and Jr. "who made us cry." Later when the house was occupied by the Althertons, it was "Ricky with his senseless animal temper" who destroyed the Willow tree. In the secure grid around the young girl's home, it is boys who act, who make senseless violence, and who, in the end, destroy the very structure of her world.

"Willow Game" ends with the narration of two events that make final sense of the story. Neither fits in the time of the rest of the story, yet both reflect upon that time. The first event is related in a flashback, back to a more recent past than the death of the Willow tree:

> Much later, after the death of the Willow, I was walking to school when a young boy came up to me and punched me in the stomach. I doubled over, crawled back to Sister Elaine's room, unable to tell her of my recent attack, unprovoked, thoughtless, insane. What could I say to her? To my mother and father? What can I say to you? All has

been told. The shreds of magic living, like the silken green ropes of the Willow's branches, dissolved about me, and I was beyond myself, a child no longer. I was filled with immense sadness, the burning of snow in a desert land of consistent warmth. (63)

The second event is related outside the time of the story, in the present: "Today I walked outside and the same experience repeated itself; oh, no the same forms, but yes, the attack. I was the same child, you see . . . " (63). It is an important *today,* for it locates the repeated attack in the time of the present narration.[2] It also offers a reason for the narration: the attack as an adult recalls the attack as a child, and the present is read in line with the past. Chronological sequence and narration confer meaning both because of the connections they make and because of the fact of connecting. After this, the story continues its narration of the present, telling of the planting of a new willow tree and describing a new spatial order: "The Apricot tree died; the Marking-Off tree is fruitless now, relieved from its round of senseless birthings. This willow tree is new, with its particular joys. It stands in the center of the block . . . between . . . " (63).

In "Willow Game" two narrative bits fall out of the temporal sequence and conclude the story. As they do they make a point about narration and time and meaning and violence. "Willow Game" posits that meaning can be construed spatially or temporally. The meaning derived from the narration of sequential events is, however, violent and senseless in the spatially oriented world of the young girl. Story itself is the sequence of violence. It is a knowledge, and it moves a child, crossing her over the threshold of adulthood. The meaning derived from the description of spatial relationships is that of contiguity. It envisions connections, proximity, geometry rather than the sequence of incident. Continuity is also a knowledge and can also afford the crossing from innocence: "I was a child before there was a South. That was before the magic of the East, the beckoning North, or the West's betrayal" (56).

In "Willow Game" narration is order of violence. To tell the story of oneself is to place in temporal order violent acts against the body and a violent act against a tree. Narration is itself the story of violence.

Spatial relationships, on the other hand, extend body to house to tree. To make sense from point in space to point in space is to locate home, to know where the body is when violent events happen.

Part Two

For Zeta Acosta the blood site is Los Angeles. His is a story that moves from his first novel, *The Autobiography of a Brown Buffalo,* to his second and last novel, *The Revolt of the Cockroach People.*³ The story traces the movement of a body searching for sense. The transition between the books is accompanied by the physical movement west, from Texas to California. *Brown Buffalo* ends with the narrator leaving El Paso in search of the Chicano homeland; *Cockroach People* begins with his arrival at a riot in Los Angeles.

The move from El Paso to Los Angeles is significant in the geometry of Chicano space. It traces movement from the center to the western end point according to an arrangement of space along the lines of a cross. El Paso is the center point of the cross. It is *El Paso del Norte;* along the north–south axis, it is the crossing point between the United States and Mexico. And with Ciudad Juárez, it is a single city cut by a river and by national politics. It is a crossing point in time too, for if we trace an origin of chicanismo in the pachuco, then El Paso is the Chicano birthplace. The southern point of the cross is Mexico City, for it was the destination of the Aztecs who ventured south from Aztlán. It is also the site where the San Patricio brigade were either hanged or branded by the U.S. Army for having deserted and sided with Mexico during the Mexican–American war. The northern extreme is Chicago, the inhospitable, white realm of the dead the Aztecs called Mictlán. It is the "Chi-town" of "Ghost Talk," where "Bigoted North Americans who forget where their grandparents came from say, Why don't you go back to *your* country."

The east–west axis is the border. From El Paso it extends to the Gulf of Mexico, a river known as the Rio Grande in the United States and as the Rio Bravo in Latin America. Its end point is Brownsville, where Juan Nepomuceno Cortina waged guerrilla warfare against yanqui conquerors. From El Paso west, the border is a fence, cleaving not only the United States and Mexico but Alta and Baja Californias. Los Angeles lies at the terminus of the western line. In time, too, it marks the end point of Mexico: Los Angeles is the site of the last battle in the U.S. conquest of northern Mexico. El Pueblo de Nuestra Señora la Reina de los Angeles lies at the end of the birth line of Chicanos. Pachucos may have been born in El Paso, but it is in Los Angeles where Chicano culture became most defined. And it has been a definition outlined in violence, from the Zoot Suit riots, to the Chicano Moratorium, to the Los Angeles Riots after Rodney King, in which the *majority* of people arrested were hispanos (though I think few Andalusians or Argentines).

Brown Buffalo begins with the body: "I stand naked before the mirror. Every morning of my life I have seen that brown belly from every angle" (11). It begins with a narration of the body, but it and narration itself are rendered problematic, for the body is uncontrollable and representation is suspect:

> I strain to vomit, pushing upward with my diaphragm, with as total control of the belly as any good clarinet player could have . . . but nothing comes except gurgling convulsions from down under. . . .
>
> "Jesus Christ, not even my body obeys me anymore!"
>
> But who really knows? Who can say for sure what causes ulcers? At the age of twenty-one six (6) different doctors showed me pictures of what they claimed were holes in my stomach. (12)

The novel continues in a narration that tries to make sense of the body, that tries to make sense through narration, an endeavor whose ability to represent reality is suspect.

The move toward sense is narrated in the move back home, to the birthplace of the body, to El Paso. The search to define the body leads back to its source. Once there, however, the narrator finds that knowledge is allocentric, residing neither in the body of the self nor at its origin. He therefore turns his search for self-definition toward the most concentrated site of chicanismo, toward Los Angeles. The necessity of this realization comes to him violently in response to hearing word of the Chicano Movement for the first time:

The bomb explodes in my head. Flashes of lightning. Stars in my eyes. I see it all before me. That is exactly what the gods have in store for me. Of course, why didn't I think of it first? I thank him, I praise him and I beg him to send me fifty bucks immediately. I will take the Greyhound to Los Angeles, call my cousin Manuel and have him put me up for a few days until I get the story from, who'd you say, the Brown Berets? God damn, why didn't I think of that? (251)

He plans the speech he'll deliver to the Chicano militants in Los Angeles. It is a speech that distrusts the politics of language and of identity yet advocates both:

> Ladies and gentlemen . . . my name is Oscar Acosta. My father is an Indian from the mountains of Durango. Although I cannot speak his language . . . you see, Spanish is the language of our conquerors. English is the language of our conquerors. . . . No one ever asked me or my brother if we wanted to be American citizens. . . . They stole our land and made us half-slaves. They destroyed our gods and made us bow down to a dead man who's been strung up for 2000 years. . . . Now what we need is, first to give ourselves a new name. We need a new identity. A name and a language all our own. . . . I propose we call ourselves . . . the Brown Buffalo people. (253)

Brown Buffalo ends with two paragraphs that announce, and seem to belong in, the next novel. In them, the narrator arrives in Los Angeles, the western end of the Chicano universe, the city "where it all happened/happens." That *Brown Buffalo* concludes in California, oddly enough, makes the story end where it started, for it began in San Francisco. But it ends in Los Angeles, and with these words, it jumps across space and books to the *Revolt of the Cockroach People:*

> We were in Los Angeles. The most detestable city in the world. Soon I'd be at my cousin Manuel's house in East L.A., the home of the biggest herd of brown buffalos in the entire world. We would eat tortillas and refried beans and talk of old times in Riverbank . . . and some time later I would become Zeta, the world-famous Chicano Lawyer who helped start the last revolution – but that, as old Doc Jennings would say, is another story. (255)

That story explodes in the opening of *Revolt of the Cockroach People*. A riot develops from the Chicano demonstration at the celebration of Christmas mass by the Cardinal in Los Angeles. As in *Brown Buffalo*, the story begins with Zeta's body beyond control. As the protestors are beaten by the police, Zeta walks unscathed: he is neither beaten nor arrested. The police do not touch him because he is the protestors' lawyer. The difference between the two novels in this matter of control over the body is one of orientation: in *Brown Buffalo*, control was a problem for the individual; in *Cockroach People*, control is exercised, or not, among others. The move from El Paso to Los Angeles, from birth to communal action, has been accompanied by a shift in narrative focus. The matter of finding meaning is moved from the story of home to the story of revolution. It is as if the first venture, the narration of the origin, had proved unable to articulate meaning. It is as if another venture, another sort of narrative line, is propounded as replacement. *Brown Buffalo* concluded, but did not sufficiently provide meaning because a narration of the self undertaken as the search for origin proved untenable. Not only did continuity of self come up short, but the neat contiguity of home did as well. In *Brown Buffalo* there is a home grid reminiscent of the triangle of "Willow Game": "Riverbank is divided into three parts, and in my corner of the world there were only three kinds of people: Mexicans, Okies, and Americans. Catholics, Holy Rollers, and Protestants. Peach pickers, cannery workers and clerks" (96). In *Revolt of the Cockroach People*, on the other hand, that narration structured by continuity and contiguity is supplanted by a response to history and place, as if in an attempt to forge a collective definition. In response to a demand in court to define *Chicano*, the narrator states:

> Unlike the black American who *cannot* return to Africa, the mother country, the Chicano is within his *own* mother country. The international border at Juarez, at Tijuana, at Nogales, at Laredo . . . these lines are but reminders to the Chicanos of what their grandparents did to them. . . . It was their own presidents, their own generals, who sold both the land and the people thereon to the United States Government for something like sixteen million dollars. (237–8)

Borderlines, narrative lines, blood lines: "these lines are but reminders to the Chicanos of what their grandparents did to them."

Just because the Viet Cong or the Chicanos temporarily lay down
their arms doesn't prove shit. For me personally, this is a kind of
end. And a beginning. But who cares about that? I was just one of a
bunch of Cockroaches that helped start a revolution to burn down
a stinking world. And no matter what kind of end this is, I'll still
play with matches.

It's in the blood now. And not only my blood. Somebody still
has to answer for Robert Fernandez and Roland Zanzibar. Somebody still has to answer for all the smothered lives of all the fighters
who have been forced to carry on, chained to a war for Freedom
just like a slave is chained to his master. Somebody still has to pay
for the fact that I've got to leave friends to stay whole and human,
to survive intact, to carry on the species and my own Buffalo run as
long as I can. (280)

Body, blood, home, revolution.

I conclude with the consideration of the move between two other
books, Charley Trujillo's *Soldados: Chicanos in Viet Nam* and *Dogs from
Illusion*.[4] These are narratives of violence, not the violence of the
threat with a gun, the punch in the belly, nor the riot in church, but
war. *Soldados* describes itself as "narratives of the Viet Nam War."
Trujillo edited this collection of testimonies by Chicano homeboys,
including himself, all of whom left for Viet Nam and returned home
to Corcoran, California. *Dogs* is a novel, the story of three Chicanos
who go to Viet Nam and return home to Illusion, a town much like
Corcoran. The testimony in the first book narrates reality: the stories
are accounts of what happened, the violence is real. The second book
tells the story from home in California through intense experiences in
Viet Nam and finally back. *Dogs* is fiction, and there, home is an
illusion.

Soldados comprises nineteen narratives; Trujillo's "Mutiny" is the
sixteenth. Trujillo presents events in his life that took place during his
tour of Viet Nam, from January to July 1970. The story is presented as
the relation of reality, and narrative serves the function of mirroring

what happened, of presenting real events in the correct sequence. The *where* that that reality happened, Viet Nam, however, is surreal or perhaps hyperreal but nonetheless, other worldly. In describing a soldier's life before Viet Nam, Trujillo states casually, "He had been a highway patrolman back in the world" (157). Home was the world, someplace other, back in time and back in space. In Viet Nam, events made no sense, "Time, space, and perception were no longer what they used to be, or pretended to be" (155). And the narration of the time and place of Viet Nam is full of violence and empty of sense:

> But the CO, out of his glory-seeking mentality, ordered a direct assault which led to more wounded and deaths than there should have been. He was such an idiot that he even wanted one of the guys to stab one of the dead Vietnamese with his bayonet in order to declare that he had stabbed him.
>
> In the wake of this, I ran up and began shooting at the dead Vietnamese in the holes, just as I had seen in the Hollywood movies. As I did this, some captain on a track started giving me some bull. I was feeling pretty strange and he didn't know how close he came to getting shot. One of the dead Vietnamese had his body buried upside down in a hole with one of his legs sticking up. I tried to pull him by his leg to see if he had any money and the leg started to come off, so I stopped pulling on it. Then someone threw a face at me. That's how bad some of the North Vietnamese had been blown up by the grenades. (156)

There beyond the world, the point to point movement of the story is that of walking point, breaking bodies into parts and trying to keep one's own body whole and return home.

Dogs begins in the sugar beet fields outside Illusion and ends there. Three friends (Ese, Chuco, and Machete) are conscripted and go off to fight in Viet Nam. The adventures in *Dogs* come after those presented in *Soldados;* they follow as fiction after testimony. But the fictionality of the novel comes after the senseless reality of *Soldados.* In both cases there is violence rather than sense, and narrative comes to signify the sequence of violence. A fictive episode in *Dogs* can make as little sense in the real world as do the real events presented in *Soldados:*

Machete then cuts the piece of rope that is holding the prisoner's head up and the chin drops to his chest. He takes an extremely sharp machete and decapitates the prisoner. The head falls like a bowling ball. He picks up the head and says, "Chihuahua, this head is heavier than I thought." Then he throws it up with both hands toward the basket and the head falls through the hoop. "Two points, motherfuckers," he says malevolently. (104)

Throughout *Dogs*, home remains elusive. It is deferred to the past and separated in space from Viet Nam. It is repeatedly recalled as the *world* where time and space were what they were supposed to be. And in the violent times and violent space of men at war, home is often recalled as the world of women. Home is the site of sense and the site where women remained. At moments when the present and local chaos seemed overwhelming, the Chicana body was recalled in an attempt to connect home. Sometimes the connection is physical, as in the talisman of pubic hairs Ese carries, at other times it as an image to keep alive. In one episode, Chuco is unable to reach his wounded and dying friend, Ro-Ro, but tries to keep him from passing out by evoking the memory of his girlfriend:

> "[A]cuerdate de las nalgotas de Nena que te esperan en Mexicali."
> "¿Orale buey, como sabes que Nena has a big butt?" complains Ro-Ro.
> "You've only shown us her picture a million times. No te apures, I won't let the gooks get to you cuñado," Chuco reassures him as he lets out a burst of machine gun fire. (181)

At one point, Ese and four others come across a group of Viet Cong, surprise them, and attack. Afterward,

> They find that all but one of the Vietnamese are dead. A female is wounded and seems to be dying. The soldiers look at one another thinking the same thing that Cadillac verbalizes, "Get it before it gets cold." Though all are tempted to rape the woman, no one does. Three Bears shoots her dead instead. An exalted feeling of accomplishment and vengeance fills the GIs, except for Marlon. Ese asks Marlon, "How come you didn't shoot?"

"No quiero matar a nadie. Nada más me quiero ir para casa,"
says Marlon without apology.

"What'd he say?" asks Cadillac.

"He says that he doesn't want to kill anyone. He just wants to go
home," answers Ese.

"I no like to kill," says Marlon. (94)

Back in the world things would be different. There would be less
violence and in its place, sense. The body could be whole and alive,
not subject to violent control. The soldiers envision the end of their
tour of duty as the end of a senseless story. But in the final vignette of
Dogs, "Last Episode: Home to Illusion," Ese, Chuco, and Machete
return home to the sugar beet fields and home to an illusion. After
surviving and killing for the United States, Ese is hassled by the
Border Patrol and beaten.

The move from home and back again in testimonial and fictive
narrative is a line written in blood. The home that was the real world
is ultimately illusory. What can one say of a home in which twice as
many soldiers who died in Viet Nam took their own lives after
returning to it? It is an illusion; it is riot in the church, the talk of ghost
and the death of tree. The story of home is a violent recounting; it is
the ordering of blood.

The End

Narrative is itself the line that establishes the authority of the line. It
defines border; it structures history; it confirms home. Narratives are
like flags, banderas, in a poem of Francisco X. Alarcón with that
name:

> Banderas
> trapos
> imbéciles
> empapados
> en sangre[5]

Late Epic, Post Postmodern

Time, Genre, Subject

I turn now to matters of time and genre and to their influence on the subject. At this point and in this moment, I accept *subject* in a sense that requires some overlap of ontology and discursivity, so that at minimum subjectivity requires a body and articulation. I also posit the acceptance now of what might be termed a Western faith in literary history, so that in setting aside certain doubts, such as the existence of time or of the subject itself, it becomes easy to conceive subjectivity (a body articulating and articulated) as a process subject to the orders of literature and history, subject to, for example, the order of genre.[1]

The notion and order of literary genres are, of course, central to Western civilization. If we allow that writing and speaking (as well as reading and listening) are modes of subject articulation, then it follows that if a case is to be made for the authority of a generic order, that sense of order can be drawn from literary and speech genres. Genres organize writing into subsets of styles, each identified by a characteristic arrangement of content and form, so that identity is constructed by adherence to an order. This process defines the literary subset, whether it be rigidly defined and traditional, whether new or hybrid, or whether something else altogether.[2]

While these literary stylistic definitions may come to us from Aristotle, the notion of speech genres that I employ here comes to us recently from Bakhtin.[3] In this sense speech genres are the subsets of utterances, the various discourses that are defined by content and form, and that both constitute and reflect different social relationships. In a way it is possible to understand the literary genre, say the epic, as similar in its relation to literature as a whole, as is a speech genre, say military speech or religious discourse, in relation to utterances as a whole. And just as the epic can be considered to shape consciousness, that is, to inform subjectivity, so too can religious speech.

And in keeping with the logic of history, genres exist in time; they have history; they contaminate and are contaminated by the zeitgeist. As historically defined sets and as extant discursive styles, literary and speech genres function both as rule and as means. They represent past tradition with which present articulation negotiates subjectivity. Subjectivity is shaped by genre, by the relation of articulation to tradition. This is the case with the notion of the national subject. There are times when a national subjectivity replicates the content and the form, the expectations and beliefs, the values, sense and meaning of the national history and mythology. There are other times when national subjectivity envisions itself a projection, a natural extension along a historical trajectory. There are also moments of rupture with tradition, times when the relations with history and myth are characterized by irony, catechresis, by revolution.

With this as the point of departure I wish to consider the subject of nation. I ground this in specific texts, beginning, for example, with *La Historia de la Nueva Mexico* by Gaspar Pérez de Villagrá, an epic of 1610. It is an epic but one that appears late, appearing at a time when the epic had been ironicized. I also look at fairly recent Chicano poetry that is epic in tendency, that is, poetry that is not specifically epic but that manifests what I understand to be the tendency that supports nationalism. Both examples, Villagrá and the Chicanos, participate in the formation of the national subject, and in both instances, genre and time are significant mitigating factors. The poems occur at crucial times, at moments when radical shifts of consciousness were taking place. They work toward defining a people amidst moments of great change.

What follows is a consideration of genre at moments of change. At the cusp of the fifteenth and sixteenth centuries, and that of the twentieth and twenty-first centuries, poetry was at work making subjects.

Epic Time

Las armas y el varon heroico canto,
El ser, valor, prudencia, y alto esfuerço,
De aquel cuya paciencia no rendida,
Por un mar de disgustos arrojada,
A pesar de la invidia poconosa,
Los hechos y prohezas un encumbrando,
De aquellos Españoles valerosos,
Que en la Occidental India remontados,
Descubriendo del mundo lo que esconde,
Plus Ultra con braveza van diziendo . . . ,
　　　　　　　　　　(Gaspar Pérez de Villagrá,
　　　　　La Historia de la Nueva Mexico, 1.1–10)

Arma virumque cano, Troiae qui primus ab oris
Italiam fato profugus Laviniaque venit
litora, multum ille et terris iactatus et alto
vi superum saevae memorem Iunonis ob iram,
multa quoque et bello passus, dum conderet urbem
inferretque deos Latio, genus unde Latinum
Albanique patres atque altae moenia Romae.
　　　　　　　　　　(Virgil, *Aeneid*, 1.1–7)[4]

　　Upon confronting a new world, Spanish explorers and conquistadors confronted radical alterity with familiar texts in hand. When Columbus ventured west beyond the edges of European maps, he interlarded himself between the lines and in the margins of his copy of Marco Polo's travels. When Hernán Cortés needed to describe a new island west of Mexico, he turned to a current chivalric romance for a name. Columbus and Cortés put into practice an advocacy for the Spanish language advanced by Antonio de Nebrija in 1492, "language has always been the companion of empire."[5] Words in the literature and language of the Old World served to guide conquest and colonialism as texts in which could be inserted paratext, from which could be derived definition, and to which could be appended story.

　　Back home, *cartas de relación* had a big impact on the Old World.[6]

The letters of Columbus and Cortés shook Europe's notion of the world and in so doing participated in the radical shift in consciousness of the early modern. Columbus and Cortés were not only men of letters but men of deeds. Their letters entered into the corpus of Spanish literature with special cachet: they were letters that claimed to relate true acts. Their relación came to signify not only the representation of reality but its narration by an active participant. The acts of encounter and the texts of the conquest entered into the literature of Spain and Europe as an important continuation: Columbus and Cortés derive meaning from the texts of Marco Polo and *Amadis de Gaula,* and both supplement that meaning with the relación. They alter the meaning of world, and they alter the meaning of self forever after. They provide key texts for the project of the Spanish Empire and for it new subject.

At the times that their texts appeared, the style and content of the cartas de relación were particularly efficacious in bridging an older world view with a new. The narrative of Marco Polo and the romance of Amadis de Gaula simultaneously provided points of origin and of departure for Columbus and Cortés, that is, the older texts at once inspired the acts of imperialism and provided meaningful context. The revolutionary perspective that Columbus and Cortés provided remained, nevertheless, rooted in a distant world view. So while imperialism provided the social texts for a rewriting of the world, it was inaugurated on a cusp, marked by the Spanish discovery of America, and was therefore conceived by the world views prevalent before discovery. This trace remains a marker of the chronotope of that conception, a genealogy of the factors at play when and where the new writing took place. In this way, later projects undertaken by others could draw upon the Spanish context in ways that the Spanish themselves could not: it is ironic, but because the Spanish essentially invented the New World, they themselves remained bound to a perspective of the Old. Other imperialist projects, particularly the British, were free to conceive their endeavors after the Spanish, that is, in an imperialist tradition. Gayatri Spivak feels the Spanish imperial text has less impact today than does the British, because of later material and ideological conditions.[7] In short, the texts that construct subjectivity are bound with a textualization that extends to the prior and the subsequent, that carries trace and creates meaning for the future.

One century after 1492, Spain pushed its empire to the extreme north of Nueva España and undertook the conquest of New Mexico. It had been a crucial century: a new world came into being, the Spanish Empire extended from California to Tierra del Fuego, great wealth had been obtained, and the most severe genocide in history had transpired.[8] The imperial century began in a single year of great changes. Beyond the work of Columbus, 1492 brought the formation of modern Spain with the consolidation of Castile and Aragon; the final defeat of the Moors and the end of eight centuries of Moslem occupation; the expulsion of Moors and Jews; the election of a Spanish pope; and Nebrija's dictionary, the first of a modern European language. It was a year of great redefinition, where each of the contributing factors participated in shaping the sense of Spain and Spaniard and participated in constructing nation, empire, and the Spanish subject.

At the end of that century, Spanish conquistadors extended the empire into New Mexico. Juan de Oñate followed the example of the conquest of the Aztecs in Mexico by Cortés (1519–21) and conquered the Pueblos in New Mexico (1598–1610). As he did, Oñate, as had Cortés before, accompanied the acts of imperialism with acts of language. One of the first acts was theatrical: Oñate's conquistadors performed the first European-language theater in the present-day United States. One of the conquistadors began narrating their exploits in a poem, an epic of relación. The *Historia de la Nueva Mexico* by Gaspar Pérez de Villagrá relates the story of empire in a genre traditionally suited to the task, but by 1610, when it was published, times had so changed that its relation was rendered ironic.

The *Historia de la Nueva Mexico* announces its place within the tradition of the epic in the opening line. "Las armas y el varon heroico canto" recalls the first line of the *Aeneid*, "Arma virumque cano." For Villagrá, as well as for others, such as Ariosto and Tasso, the *Aeneid* provided the prime example of the epic, the form and content after which they wrote. Ariosto begins *Orlando Furioso*, "Le donne, i cavillier, l'arme, gli amori / le cortesie, l'audaci imprese io canto" and

Tasso begins *Gerusalemme liberata,* "Canto l'arme pietose e 'l cap-
itano." *Orlando Furioso* (1516) and *Gerusalamme liberata* (1579) span the
century that for the Spanish Empire extended from Columbus to
Oñate. *Orlando Furioso, Gerusalemme liberata,* and the *Historia de la
Nueva Mexico* share temporal distance from the *Aeneid* and share having been written in the vernacular. In this, all three participate in the
development of modern European national subjects from the medieval remnants of Rome, especially as it progressed after 1492.

That century for the Spanish Empire may have been shared by
the rest of Europe but for Spain the times were particularly acute.
Nowhere else did events consolidating the nation and giving birth
to empire so densely coalesce as they did in Spain in 1492. Because
of this, the Spanish national and imperial contexts provided sharply
defined meaning for the letters and epics of relación. The Spanish
national and imperial subject emerged better defined and earlier
than did the subjects of Italy or of the rest of modern Europe. This
was due to the chronotope in 1492, to the factors of language,
literature, and politics at play. This particular set of factors, absent
from the contexts of Ariosto or Tasso, provides a context that the
Historia de la Nueva Mexico shares with the epic of Chile, *La
Araucana.*[9] Published in 1569, Alonso Ercilla y Zuñiga's epic narrated the conquest of the southern extreme of the Spanish Empire.[10] Yet despite the close similarity with the epic of New Mexico (1610), the *Araucana* appeared in the midst of a sufficiently
different chronotope so as to have a very different impact.

The *Historia de la Nueva Mexico* gains meaning in part because of its
genre, because of the meaning epic had accrued at the time of the
Renaissance, the rebirth in Western consciousness of the early modern. Virgil, as had Homer, but especially Virgil for Romance peoples,
had come to signify for the makers of the New World, the classical
order of the Old. The *Aeneid* exemplified the generic order of the
great classical empire. It marked the classical form of relación, so that
any subsequent epic narration could bear the trace of classical antiquity. Because the genre, the word "epic" itself, had come to signify
greatness, that the *Historia de la Nueva Mexico* comes after the *Aeneid*
means that it followed, and followed as, a great narration. The *Historia*

also takes on further generic meaning, for epic had come to signify not only the form of the great story but the form of the national/ imperial text as well. The epic had come to stand as the prime genre for narrating a people, a nation, and had come to do so long before the genre we would recognize today as history.[11] It stood as the genre to represent national reality and to narrate the story of the nation's most heroic acts. The story of the *Aeneid* defined the Roman subject by narrating the great exploits of men. In other words, it promulgated a genre whose order very clearly identified what was worthy of narration, what kinds of acts by men forged the nation.

Orlando Furioso, Gerusalemme liberata, the *Araucana,* and the *Historia de la Nueva Mexico* all accrue this meaning of genre. All are great poems that tell great stories. They relate the types of stories prescribed by the genre: they are full of masculine violence, conquest, of venturing out and defeating an alien other. In this they define a people in the narration of highly selected acts, specifically in the encounter with the outsider. The *Iliad* and the *Aeneid* had come to signify classical antiquity for the early modern and had become a prescription for defining the self. For the early modern, the nation and the national subject were defined in the epic narration of great men defeating alien others. To this prescription the four epics in the vernacular, Italian and Spanish, subscribe.

By following the *Aeneid,* generally by generic formula and specifically by opening-line allusion, the later epics locate themselves in a temporal trajectory of meaning, acknowledging precedent and genre, form and sense. The vernacular epics mark themselves as subsequent manifestations of the formula and impulse espoused by the classic epic more than a millennium and a half earlier. The direct references to the *Aeneid* supplement the meaning accrued, for the later epics do not merely obtain a gloss of classicism, they locate themselves very clearly as heirs to a well-defined tradition. In that they follow in time along an envisioned line of cultural progression, they follow the tendency of the genre to write the subject according to a particular ordering of axiology, aesthetics, epistemology.

This epic tendency organizes the production of meaning by providing a frame of reference of exemplary texts and generic order. It imbues texts according to a tradition of meaning, when by necessity they are marked by varying degrees of difference: *Gerusalemme liberata* and the *Historia,* for example, are shaped by the *Aeneid* even though neither is contemporary with it nor written in Latin. This continuity yet difference was of course quite significant for the subject of Europe in the early modern period, during the shifts in consciousness of the Renaissance from, roughly, the invention of perspective in painting through the life of Shakespeare. In moments of great change, the sense of continuity the epic offered could combine with the rule of genre to provide not only the means to read change but meaning itself. The epic of the *Aeneid* could make sense of new languages, such as Italian and Spanish, or of new lands, such as New Mexico or Chile.

The epic tendency carries its effects not only among diverse examples of the epic but among generic variations as well. Right around 1492, two chivalric romances appear in Spain: *Tirant lo Blanch* appears in Catalan in 1490, and *Amadis de Gaula,* which is actually much older, begins a rapid succession of printings in Castilian in 1508. Along with the likes of *Orlando Furioso,* they are written not in a classical language but in the vernacular and contribute to the legitimation of the vernacular as a literary language. Beyond this, they also contribute to a generic variation that would eventually lead to the novel. Changes such as these – linguistic, literary, and generic changes – were complicit in the development of the modern European subject. So while the trace of the *Aeneid* was still present and the epic tendency still evident, the chivalric romance in the new languages of the European nations did mark a break of sorts with the past, a paradigmatic shift that corresponded with a new paradigm of the world. In the times of altering paradigms, of metaphoric change, of *Gerusalemme liberata* standing for the *Aeneid,* Castilian for Latin, the chivalric romance for the epic, and New Mexico for Troy, in those times, the epic tendency and trace of the *Aeneid* provided a continuity of meaning, an ordered linearity perceived in retrospect. In essence, the order of metonymy could be called upon to ascribe meaning in times of metaphoric change: continuity in times of change.

Spanish Time

Gaspar Pérez de Villagrá acted, as conquistador and as poet, at the end of Spain's remarkable century. The 1598 conquest of New Mexico is defined and textualized twelve years later: simultaneously in 1610, the crown names New Mexico a royal colony and Villagrá's epic is published. The conquest occurs late in the history of Spanish imperial expansion in the New World, and the publication of the *Historia* also occurs late, in some ways too late, in the history of the genre. Oñate's conquest of New Mexico was already a late act of conquest, working north from New Spain, from Old Mexico. His project was conquest, not, as had been that of Cabeza de Vaca, exploration, nor, as was to be that of Junipero Serra, colonization. Oñate followed in the steps of Cortés and sought to conquer another realm for the empire. For Spain, having Cortés and Columbus for comparison, Oñate's conquest seemed secondary, derivative, late, and slight. For greater Europe, too, New Mexico by 1598 was already an old story. A relación of the 1583 expedition of Antonio de Espejo, which claimed to have discovered, and to have given name to, New Mexico, was rapidly disseminated across Europe in three languages: it was published in Madrid and Paris in 1586 and in London in 1587.[12]

Be this as it may, Oñate did have with him Gaspar Pérez de Villagrá, a poet who would write an epic of relación and narrate the conquest of New Mexico in the fashion of the great genre. Oñate may have made it in time to conquer the vast northern territory for the empire, but the epic of his conquest appeared too late to be taken without irony. The genre was already old when the *Araucana* and *Gerusalemme liberata* appear. The epic's capacity to narrate a people was already being supplanted by the emerging genres of history and the novel that were to flourish in the modern period. But on the cusp of the early modern, and particularly so in Spain around 1492, the epic could yet survive as a viable, if archaic, form for "literal" relación. Because the transition was so abrupt for Spain, the former modes of understanding remained in close proximity, still useful for some time after the radical shift. The *Poema Mio Cid,* written about 1140, for example, could still serve as the national epic, especially since the medieval epic recounted a story once again current in 1492: the defeat of the Moors and the consolidation of Christian Spain.

Within the brief span between Oñate's conquest in 1598 and the publication of Villagrá's epic in 1610, there took place in Spain a most consequential event that had profound ramifications for the Spanish subject and for the West in general. In 1605 *Don Quixote* was published. It was to have tremendous impact immediately and not only on Spanish letters. It appeared in Spanish in two parts in 1605 and 1615. It was immediately disseminated in translation, first in the English version of Thomas Shelton (*The history of the valerous and wittie knight-errant don Quixote of the Mancha,* London, 1612), then in the French of César Oudin (*L'ingénieux don Quixote de la Manche,* Paris, 1614) and the Italian of Lorenzo Franciosini de Castelfiorentino (*L'ingengnoso cittadino don Chisciotte della Mancia,* Venice, 1622). Success was so quick that before Cervantes came out with part two, his novel was the best seller in London. But the popularity in translation did not match that in Spanish, in which during its first year *Don Quixote* was published four times, twice in Madrid and twice furtively in Lisbon and in Valencia. *Don Quixote* became the prime text defining the Spanish character, both reflecting and forging Spanish subjectivity, and supplanted other texts such as *Poema Mio Cid.* It had a profound impact on Western literature by defining, as it did, the novel and by relying so heavily on irony. *Don Quixote* radically altered Spanish reading so that after it, the epic of Oñate's heroics was read ironically. The rules changed so markedly in 1605 that publication of the *Historia* seemed a case of particularly bad timing.

The changes that *Don Quixote* precipitated for the European subject can be evidenced, according to Erich Auerbach and Robert Alter, in the changes in the order of character and the order of genre.[13] Both Auerbach and Alter argue that at the time of *Don Quixote,* and at least partially due to it, Western consciousness broke with the premodern and moved to the early modern. In *Mimesis: The Representation of Reality in Western Literature,* Auerbach contrasts the problems of reality for two characters, Don Quixote and Hamlet. The madness of each marks a new level of introspection for the Western subject, a distant reflection of the self, a psychological depth, an irony. This is evident to a degree in *Don Quixote:*

> Seldom, indeed, has a subject suggested the problematic study of contemporary reality as insistently as does Don Quixote. The ideal conceptions of a past epoch, and of a class which has lost its functions, in conflict with the reality of the contemporary present ought to have led to a critical and problematic portrayal of the latter, the more so since the mad Don Quixote is often superior to his normal opponents by virtue of his moral steadfastness and native wit. But Cervantes did not elaborate his work in this direction. (332–3)

Shakespeare, however, did seem to elaborate where Cervantes did not:

> Among the Spanish authors of the golden age whom I know, Cervantes is certainly the one whose characters come nearest to being problematic. But if we want to understand the difference, we need only compare the bewildered, easily interpreted, and ultimately curable madness of Don Quixote with Hamlet's fundamental and many-faceted insanity which can never be cured in this world. Since the pattern of life is so fixed and secure, no matter how much that is wrong may occur within it, we feel in the Spanish works, despite all their colorful and lively bustle, nothing of a movement in the depths of life, or even of a will to explore it in principle and recast it in practice. (332)

What Auerbach finds more fully developed by Shakespeare than by Cervantes is the problematic relationship of protagonist to reality. These problems with reality manifest in the characters' madness. The insanity of Hamlet is greater than that of Don Quixote because he faces a reality where the pattern of life is less fixed. While Auerbach clearly locates the problem with reality in the order of character, he nevertheless hints at the significance of the order of genre. He observes of Cervantes but does not elaborate: "His representation of Spanish reality is dispersed in many individual adventures and sketches; the bases of that reality remain untouched and unmoved" (333).

In *Partial Magic: The Novel as a Self-Conscious Genre,* Robert Alter places the self-consciousness of *Don Quixote* not so much in the working of character as in the structure of the novel:

> The novel begins out of an erosion of belief in the authority of the written word and it begins with Cervantes. It fittingly takes as the initial target of its literary critique the first genre to have enjoyed popular success because of the printing press – the Renaissance chivalric romance. Although novelists were by no means the first – and Cervantes of course the first among them – to see in the mere fictionality of fictions the key to the predicament of a whole culture, and to use this awareness centrally in creating new fictions of their own. (3)

While Auerbach finds in Cervantes a minor dispersion of reality, Alter, on the other hand, identifies the structural irony of *Don Quixote:* it "begins out of an erosion of belief in the authority of the written word," and it sees "the mere fictionality of fictions." Structural irony pervades *Don Quixote:* the prologue's address of the reader, "desocupado lector," for example, distances the reader by calling attention to the fictive event of reading and to the very novelness of *Don Quixote.* This paratextual distancing is small of course compared to the narration itself, where the windmill world of the reader is far from the monster world of the character. The dramatic irony that so thoroughly informs *Don Quixote* similarly informs *Hamlet.* The reality known to the reader is not that known to either protagonist, and in the case of *Hamlet,* the "Mousetrap" functions to a limited degree the way the prologue functions in *Don Quixote.* The self-consciousness that Auerbach finds in each work may not differ so much quantitatively as qualitatively. For in *Hamlet* the main focus of the irony lies between character and reality (or character and representation of reality, or character and story), and the reader is asked to take the protagonist seriously. In *Don Quixote,* the madness of the protagonist serves to direct the main thrust of the irony, between reader and story, and the reader is asked to laugh.

In that *Don Quixote* stands recognized most often as the first modern novel, it stands as generic exemplar. And in this capacity it does something that *Hamlet* does not: it creates genre. The novel was, after all, something novel. Alter juxtaposes Cervantes with Milton in order to describe the relationship of the new genre with the break from the premodern:

> Milton is perhaps the last great moment in a tradition of mimesis that begins for Western literature with Homer and the Bible. His poem memorably represents that aspect of the Renaissance which is the conscious culmination of a continuous cultural development through two and a half millennia. Cervantes' novel, on the other hand, is one of the supreme achievements of that impulse in the Renaissance which was already moving toward the troubled horizon of modernity. Cervantes cannot share Milton's Christian-humanist confidence in the power of language and the literary tradition to adumbrate the glory of God's nature. From this point on, cultural creativity would proceed more and more through a recapitulative critique of its own past, and a major line of fiction would be avowedly duplicitous, making the paradox of its magically real duplicity one of its principal subjects. In these respects, Cervantes does not merely anticipate a later mode of imagination but fully realizes its possibilities; subsequent writers would only explore from different angles the imaginative potentialities of a kind of fiction that he authoritatively conceived. In this, as in other ways, *Don Quixote* is the archetypal novel that seems to encompass the range of what would be written afterward. Ironically reaching for the dream of a medieval world through Renaissance literary productions, it remains one of the most profoundly modern of all novels. (29)

Self-consciously standing on the cusp of the modern, *Don Quixote* inaugurates a sensibility that would remain intelligible for the modern. The irony that speaks to the modern is found not only in the mad introspection of character but also in the very order and structure of genre. Because of this, Don Quixote could remain a *modern* novel whose irony could be appreciated by Auerbach or Alter or by Eliot during his reign over English poetics at Faber and Faber.[14]

The time of Villagrá's *Historia de la Nueva Mexico* (1610) at the end of Spain's imperial century is also the time of *Don Quixote* (1605) and

Hamlet (1603) at the dawn of a particular type of ironic subjectivity that would later come to be viewed as characteristic of modernism.[15] But whereas the *Historia* subscribes to an order articulated by Virgil, the *Quixote* and *Hamlet* articulate one that would inspire Freud. Contemporaneous only chronologically, the *Historia* seems belated while the *Quixote* and *Hamlet* seem precursory, early modern. In genre and epoch, the *Historia* comes at the end of a time, at the end of Spain's most dramatic century, and at the end of a naive subjectivity that could be narrated in epics and in cartas de relación. Its orientation to the past, not simply its retrospection but its reverence to the pasts of Cortés and Virgil, aligns Villagrá's epic with the cusp of subjectivity at the beginning of Spain's imperial century. It seems a much older text than it is, sharing with Columbus, Cortés, and even with Ercilla the profound impact of 1492 and the older world view it altered. The *Historia* narrates its reality of great acts by great men according to the generic order of the epic, an order that emerges from a distant, and for the modern, nearly incomprehensible past.

Don Quixote is a novel in which the past figures prominently. The protagonist lives too late to inhabit a bygone world, the world of the chivalric romance, of Amadis de Gaula, for example. Don Quixote lives at a time when all the dragons have been killed, and *Don Quixote* is printed at a time when the conquest of the New World had transpired. The protagonist looks back to a lost age, to an enchanted time when the world was a different place. And while Don Quixote looks back, abrogating the distance with the imaginary, the reader, the "desocupado lector," delights in the irony of that temporal dislocation. Quixote is an old man whose madness transcends time, and the reader is keenly aware of the break with reality. This structural irony pervades the novel as a realization of a potential of the genre. It marks much more than the peculiarities of character and points to a fundamental irony that would color perspective to follow and would come to stand as a primary mode of modernist consciousness.

In addition, *Don Quixote* actually was something novel. It was something new in form, quite unlike poetry. While the epic may share the narration of a story with the novel, the epic, like the lyric, differs fundamentally from the novel. In his theory of the novel,

Bakhtin contrasts the poetic impulse of poetry with the tendency of the novel to articulate a novelistic discourse. Simply put, poetry strives for the unmediated, single-voiced expression of the poet. Poetry claims a transparency or immediacy or direct link between poet and poem, between intention or vision and meaning. For Bakhtin, the poem is always the monologic articulation of the single poet, speaking his or her mind, expressing sentiments and truths as far as they can be known by one. In this manner, poetic discourse is expressly suited for the task of the epic, for articulating the spirit of a people. The novel, on the other hand, invites dialogue: novelistic discourse becomes a site for the interaction of various characters speaking with various perspectives, for dispersing reality. The novelist juggles dialogue where the poet espouses "truths." Because of this, the novel differs generically from the epic and other poetry precisely here: the novel invites difference and comes to be amid different perspectives. And in this manner, the novel works in quite a different way than does the epic.[16]

Don Quixote, in story and in genre, changed time. It thoroughly undermined the primacy of poetic discourse, especially its single-voiced and unmediated presentation of poetic vision, and supplanted it with prose and ironic mediation. This meant that the *Historia de la Nueva Mexico* appeared too late, coming as it did five years after *Don Quixote,* to be able to be read as it might have been. *Don Quixote* had changed the time of the Spanish subject, and because of this, the epic *relación* of the conquest of New Mexico was read as an anachronism and rendered ironic by the changing times. After *Don Quixote,* the times were such that the *Historia* could not be taken as had the *Araucana,* that is, taken on the terms of the epic and the literal *relación.* The result was that the *Historia* was largely ignored, having nothing of the huge impact that, by contrast, the *Araucana* had.

Don Quixote spoke to the seventeenth-century Spanish subject in ways the *Historia de la Nueva Mexico* did not. The *Quixote* came to articulate the national character, postconquest, late empire, disenchanted and ironic. It would supplant the archetypes provided by Cortés, Columbus, or by *Amadis de Gaula.* The epic of Oñate never had much impact on the national character of Spain or Mexico. After all, not only was the *Historia* late, its story paled in comparison to that of Cortés and the conquest of Old Mexico. Nor does it figure in the cultural history of the United States. Its sole impact has been on New Mexico, where the epic succeeded in realizing its potential and participated in a retrospective subject making.

Chicano Times

Of all Chicanos, northern New Mexicans are perhaps the ones with the strongest sense of themselves as hispanos.[17] And this, I think, is due in part to the *Historia de la Nueva Mexico*. The factors of isolation and the early colonization preserved a subjectivity that in some ways has maintained connection with a distant past. Santa Fe, New Mexico, is second only to St. Augustine, Florida, founded in 1565, as the oldest city in the United States, which, needless to say, means that the Spanish presence in the present-day United States antedates the English. Santa Fe was the northern-most extension of the Spanish Empire for nearly two centuries until the late eighteenth-century colonization of California. Compared to the other major Chicano regions, Texas and California, New Mexico had a much longer period as part of New Spain, from colonization and the founding of Santa Fe in 1610 to New Mexican statehood in 1912 (302 years), compared to the founding of San Antonio in 1718 to Texan independence in 1835 (117 years), and San Francisco in 1776 to Californian statehood in 1848 (72 years).[18] This combines with the relatively brief period of Mexicanness, when New Mexico was part of the Mexican nation, from independence from Spain in 1821 to conquest by the United States in 1846 (25 years). It therefore becomes particularly easy for the northern New Mexican to fashion an image of self that emphasizes its Spanishness, that is, to fashion the self as hispano.[19]

This dimension of New Mexican subjectivity is rooted in cultural practice. To this day, New Mexican Spanish bears traces of the sixteenth century that are absent in the Spanish of other Chicanos as well as the Spanish of Mexicans and Spaniards. (The use of *asina* or *ansina* for the current *así* is an example.) Religious practice there is similarly marked with vestiges: the flagellation of the penitentes recalls the different world when Santa Fe was settled. New Mexican cultural practice bears links to the great Spanish century that began with Columbus and ended with Oñate. And part of New Mexican culture is the *Historia de la Nueva Mexico*. The northern New Mexicans have an early modern epic in a way that no one else does in the United States, in the way that Chile does with the *Araucana*. And on one very elemental level, possessing a Renaissance epic has had powerful consequences in orienting New Mexican subjectivity toward time past.

The *Historia de la Nueva Mexico* was read in New Mexico in ways it could not have been read in Mexico or Spain. Villagrá's relación of Oñate, the Pueblos, and Santa Fe could be taken as the local and epic truth. It could be taken as the unmediated expression of a founding father, of a conquistador and poet. Because it is the founding epic of an isolated and retrospective people, the *Historia* could be taken by New Mexicans without any of the post-*Don Quixote* irony that pervaded the Spanish-speaking world. In other words, in New Mexico the epic was allowed to have the impact of an epic: Villagrá spoke of and for the people. As a result, the New Mexican subject is both reflected in and forged by an early modern text whose content and form ascribe to a much older world view: "Las armas y el varon heroico canto, / El ser, valor, prudencia, y alto esfuerço, . . . / De aquellos Españoles valerosos, / Que en la Occidental India remontados, / Descubriendo del mundo lo que esconde, / Plus Ultra con braveza van diziendo. . . . " It is a world view of exploration and conquest, of the deeds of valiant Spaniards in the sixteenth century, of Spain's first imperial century, of an epic that reaches back to Virgil for precedent, for form, for meaning: "Arma virumque cano."

This makes northern New Mexicans different from other Chicanos. Perhaps the text that would approach the *Historia* in impact for Californian Chicanos would be the nineteenth-century corrido "Joaquín Murrieta." It differs from Villagrá's epic not only because of its late date of production, two and a half centuries after the *Historia,* but also because of generic characteristics: a corrido is quite a different verse form than the epic. The corrido would be even more central to Texas, where if it wasn't invented, at least flourished simultaneously

with its more southern Mexican counterpart. In fact, when document-
ing Texan Chicano literature, much has been made of the central
importance of the corrido of Gregorio Cortez, such as in Américo
Paredes's seminal work, *With His Pistol in His Hands*.[20] The corrido, a
highly formulaic verse form, much more rigid a form than is the epic,
descends from the Spanish romance and relates the heroics of a real
person such as Murrieta or Cortez.[21]

The Californian and Texan corridos so differ from Villagrá's *Historia* that they manifest relatively little of the *epic* effect. To begin with,
corridos are popular verse, set to music and performed: they are
much less the literary and textual artifact than is the epic. And even
though they maintain a consistency of story, the corridos by virtue of
their realization through performance are a more open form, one
that allows structurally for the alterations and adjustments of the
individual corridista. Then too, the genre itself was born in the
particular chronotope of nineteenth-century conflicts between Mexico and the United States, and to a lesser degree, between Mexico
and France. The corrido tells of Joaquín Murrieta's revenge against
the greedy gringos in California and of Gregorio Cortez's flight from
the Rangers in Texas. Its focus is Mexico versus the United States
and not, like Villagrá's, Spaniard versus Indian. The times of the
corrido and of its effects on Chicano subjectivity is the time of
Manifest Destiny, the time of U.S. imperialism and the conquest of
northern Mexico. The time of the epic is a wholly different time
with a wholly different perspective. There are corridos in New
Mexico too; there are the tales of Elfego Baca, for example, but there
are no equivalents of the *Historia* in California or Texas. And this has
contributed to the construction of a subjectivity that can read itself in
an early modern epic and trace meaning to so distant a past. It is
understandable then that in the 1960s, the Chicano movements in
California, of the Farmworkers Union and the Brown Berets, and in
Texas, of the La Raza Unida Party, had nothing similar to the land
grant movement, where northern New Mexicans claimed redress
from the United States for lands stolen from them, for lands originally granted by the king of Spain and for which they still possessed
fading, early modern parchments.

In time, the *Historia de la Nueva Mexico* had two quite different effects. For the world outside of New Mexico its impact was negligible, a product of bad timing. Within New Mexico it was read without irony, taken seriously, and incorporated into the literature of the subject. To the degree that the *Historia* speaks for and of the New Mexican hispano subject, to that degree, that subjectivity transpires bound to a former time and a former world view. In 1972, when the Chicano movement and a Chicano subjectivity were still young, Reies Tijerina sponsored a conference in Albuquerque to consolidate the movement and clarify identity politics. Tijerina, who led the New Mexican land grant movement, invited two other major proponents of differing types of chicanismo, José Angel Gutierrez from Texas and founder of the political party, La Raza Unida, and Rodolfo Corky Gonzales from Colorado and the Crusade for Justice. Gutierrez sought unity behind the identity *raza,* the *race* or *people,* especially as in the mestizo race, in a quest to forge a racialized, third-party politics. Gonzales, in his own writing and in his organizing efforts, had been implicated in use of the term *Chicano* and the homeland, *Aztlán.* Tijerina, who based New Mexican land grant claims on the colonial authority of the Spanish crown, was faced with the dilemma of wanting to maintain an hispano identity while at the same time unifying with more radical and consciously anticolonial elements. Tijerina called the conference el Congreso Indio Hispano. But for Chicanos who were sensitive to the racism in asserting a Spanish identity, Tijerina's compromise proved naive, if not insensitive, offensive.

For Tijerina, the Indio Hispanic subject accrues general meaning because of a very particular contiguous relationship: some northern New Mexicans are descendants of the very colonizers who had been granted land by the king of Spain. It is a subjectivity that comes to meaning linearly, that is, that comes to definition because of a claim to an unbroken line back to an authoritative source. Such meaning is construed upon a sense of *hispano* that is imbued with patriarchy and colonialism, that is, in short, imbued with meaning from the past time of Oñate and Villagrá. The existence of the physical artifact, the possession of the actual land grant documents, underscores the continuity that writes the New Mexican subject:

for in addition to the textual transmission of regal decree across the intervening generations, there remains the actual document itself, signed in the actual hand of the deputies of the king. And this effect of the land grant text, its participation in the formation of the subject, is similar to the effect of Villagrá's conquest epic of relación. The northern New Mexican is defined as a nation, not as a state but as a people, in part by the literal reading of colonial texts. It is a subject that reaches back to the authority and acts and texts of king and conquistador and epic poet. It is a subjectivity that comes to be, in part, in the present in the quotidian acts of valorizing a retrospective perspective.

The overriding tendency of such a nationalist subjectivity, despite Tijerina's synthetic *Indio* Hispano, is toward a narrowly defined subject articulated at the end of a narrow line. The *Historia de la Nueva Mexico* functions as a source text to which the New Mexican subject looks in retrospect for meaning, in the same manner that the epic itself looks in retrospect to the *Aeneid*. To the degree that that subjectivity is hispano, it restricts the essence of the contemporary subject to a narrow definition that can occupy the present end point of the colonial and even classical trajectory. The essential New Mexican nationalist subject can therefore be idealized as the hispano land grant holder and descendant of a conquistador. At further and further remove on the hierarchy of national subjectivity, that is, less and less in line with the authoritative line, would be the landless or more newly immigrant hispano, the mestizo, and the Indian. The tendency of this subject formation to found its sense on a literal contiguity with texts of relación manifests itself in patriarchal, postcolonial, and racist politics of self-definition.

The converse of this to a degree is the Chicano identity politics that define Chicano as Indian, denying the hispano component of mestizaje. It bases itself on a matrilinearity that ignores the rapist conquistador father. Instead of the *Historia of la Nueva Mexico,* founding texts would be the *Popol Vuh,* the poetry of Nezahualcoyotl, and countless elements of the oral tradition. This perspective has been advanced to varying degrees by many opposed to a hispano identity, from Alurista to Gloria Anzaldúa. Taken to its extreme, its most radical formulation rejects not only *hispano* but *latino* as well, rejecting any Latin American identification that descends patrilinearly from the colonizing Spaniard. For the cultural similarities that unite hispanos or latinos, such as the Spanish language and Catholicism, were introduced by the colonial fathers. The Chicano-as-indio, however, is similar to the Chicano-as-hispano in that it also proposes a subjectivity descended from one source, albeit maternal in the case of indios and paternal in the case of hispanos. This tendency toward a unitary subjectivity is similar in form but quite different in context: the historical and contemporary facts of colonialism and postcolonialism value being Indian much, much less than they value being hispano. Because of this, indio Chicanos in the United States and indio Mexicanos in Chiapas, for example, espouse a radical antihegemonic subjectivity if only because of the facts of race politics. Yet despite the huge difference in power, the tendencies of both indio and hispano chicanismos are similar in form: an idealized and unitary self that is defined by the rule of a past line.

Participating in Tijerina's Congreso Indio Hispano was Corky Gonzales, the Denver activist who had been extremely influential in Chicano identity politics. Gonzales had sponsored the 1969 youth conference that produced the Plan Espiritual de Aztlán, in many ways the birth certificate of the Chicano, and was the author of what was considered the epic poem of the Chicano movement, *I am Joaquín/Yo soy Joaquín*. In the poem, Gonzales served as the epic poet or the genius of the cultural nation, one who both related and embodied the spirit of Aztlán.[22] The cover of the 1972 Bantam Books edition declares "An epic of the Mexican American people / the most famous poem of the Chicano Movement in America" and includes a chronology, "People and events from Mexican and Mexican American History," from 3000 B.C. to 1972.[23] The focus of the epic is Joaquín Murrieta, the anti-gringo hero of the Californian corrido; but be that as it may, *I am Joaquín* never realizes the narrow focus of the *Historia de la Nueva Mexico,* of *Orlando Furioso,* or of the *Aeneid*. As Gonzales declares on the back cover of the Bantam edition, "*I am Joaquín* was the first work of poetry to be published by Chicanos for Chicanos and is the forerunner of the Chicano cultural

renaissance. . . . The sounds of movement, the literary and anthropo-
logical quest for our roots, the renewal of a fierce pride and tribal
unity, are the reasons why *I am Joaquín* had to be shared with all my
hermanos y hermanas, fathers, mothers, and grandparents. Their time,
and now our time, could not be left behind and forgotten." This,
the "epic of the Mexican American people" and the "most famous
poem of the Chicano Movement," works differently than do the
traditional epics, consciously different due to differences in the factors of time, genre, and hybridity.

Taken together as coalescence, as fusion, as interplay, time/genre/
hybridity can be the active matrix where varieties of the subject can
be understood to work out. In such a configuration, time would
mark *time,* as in chronological order and *the times,* as in epoch and
zeitgeist, and would thus form a basis for evaluating a tropic relation
to the modes of consciousness of an age. Genre would mean the
organization into style, and order the form and contents of prevalent
texts. It implies a prescriptive system of values. Hybridity would
mean simply the relative tendency to combine factors that inform
subjectivity. Thus considering the dissimilitude of the time/genre/
hybridity matrices, *I am Joaquín* can be understood to participate in a
subject formation with a wholly different orientation, a different
politics even, than does *Historia de la Nueva Mexico. I am Joaquín*
points to a Chicano subjectivity whose moment occurs at the end of
modernism and at the cusp of postmodernism, and despite its epic
qualities, it does not locate the ultimate authority for meaning in a
dead past. The *Historia* authorizes a hispano subjectivity whose meaning is deferred to former times and lost origins. *I am Joaquín* becomes
the epic of the Chicano movement at the very end of the modernist
era, an era preceded by the early modernist visions of Columbus and
Cortés and Cervantes. It comes to define chicanismo, and even
though not a radical poem, it comes to participate in a radical subjectivity. The Chicano poetry that *I am Joaquín* inspires ensues after
modernism, during the turn toward postmodernism, and quickly
eclipses Gonzales's epic.

The time/genre/hybridity matrix of the *Historia* is particularly
suited to the construction of a unified subject, to a well-defined ideal

national character. The epic participates with archaisms of language and religion and with the land grant movement to write the New Mexican national subject. That subject can look in retrospect to the early modern era for sense; it can read the *Historia* literally and without irony, and envision a nonhybridized descent from the father.[24] This is a possibility for the New Mexican subject in ways that it is not possible for other Chicanos who lack an early modern epic. *I am Joaquín,* on the other hand, has a different matrix. It is ostensibly retrospective: it defines the Chicano by citing every ancestor. And yet, while it does outline a genealogy, its focus is decidedly contemporary and with a vision toward the future.

> I am Joaquín,
> lost in a world of confusion,
> caught up in the whirl of a
> gringo society,
> confused by the rules,
> scorned by attitudes,
> suppressed by manipulation,
> and destroyed by modern society.
> My fathers
> have lost the economic battle
> and won
> the struggle of cultural survival.
> And now!
> I must choose
> between
> the paradox of
> victory of the spirit,
> despite physical hunger,
> or
> to exist in the grasp
> of American social neurosis,
> sterilization of the soul
> and a full stomach.
>
> (6–9)

The epic tendency to define the national character is a tendency of *I am Joaquín*. That it spoke for and defined the Chicano movement was in fact the reason it was considered the epic. But while it asserts the epic tendency, it is somewhat duplicitous in the realization, for *I am Joaquín* has it both ways: it defines chicanismo while at the same time it undermines its own endeavor.

> La Raza!
> Mejicano!
> Español!
> Latino!
> Hispano!
> Chicano!
> or whatever I call myself,
> I look the same
> I feel the same
> I cry
> and
> sing the same.
> I am the masses of my people and
> I refuse to be absorbed.
> I am Joaquín.
> The odds are great
> but my spirit is strong,
> my faith unbreakable,
> my blood is pure.
> I am Aztec prince and Christian Christ.
> I SHALL ENDURE!
> I WILL ENDURE!
> (98–100)

On the one hand, meaning is construed from the past: the Chicano is defined by a genealogy. But in this case the emphasis is not on linearity and proper sequence but on selection. Emphasis is furthermore on an extant subjectivity that happens to descend from diverse sources, so that meaning lies in the existing combination. In this way genealogy functions not so much to establish an authoritative line and origin as to identify the elements that combine to play in subject formation. This is then supplemented in two ways: first, subjectivity is implicated further in selection, rather than merely combinatory sequence; and second, the epic project of writing the subject is itself undermined. *I am Joaquín* not only delineates the Chicano subject "la raza, etc." but also declares "whatever I call myself, / I look the same / I feel the same / I cry / and / sing the same." That is, the subject is not only a product of selection but also unaffected by the epic definition. The subject is thus, in Bakhtin's terms, unfinalized and therefore open to further reading, writing, meaning. Both instances, selection and indefinability, project a characteristic of chicanismo that corresponds with contemporary notions of subjectivity: it is something performed rather than simply essential.

Selection implies the formation of a subject from competing paradigms of subjectivities, from, for example, the differences embodied in the names Raza, Mejicano, Español, Latino, Hispano, Chicano. Selection also implies that the subject realized in the process is itself paradigmatic. If envisioned as Hegelian dialectic, then the resulting subject of selection can be understood as a synthesis, as the higher truth made from the competing factors, from thesis and antithesis. José Vasconcelos conceives mestizaje in this way, so that la raza cósmica is a higher truth for humanity, the synthesis of the European and the American races. But if selection is understood as a Bakhtinian dialogue, then no such synthesis occurs. Instead, subjectivity is seen as the site of competing discourses, discourses possessed with different authorities. In such an active field, the subject asserts a self by employing and opposing various discourses. Both dialectic and dialogism share an emphasis on selection, which is the pole of metaphor and irony. This differs from an emphasis on combination, metonymy and synecdoche, that the *Historia de la Nueva Mexico* provides for the New Mexican hispano subject. In this case, hispano subjectivity defines itself by correct placement on the authoritative line, so that the past is not one of alternative paradigms but one of origin, source, meaning. This linear retrospect makes the hispano subjectivity a conservative one, defined by birth. A paradigmatic Chicano subjectivity, on the other hand, remains unfinalized, subject to a choosing of the self.

Indefinability manifests as a lack of faith in the relación and there-fore contributes to a concern for the responsibility for the subject. By declaring "whatever I call myself . . . ," *I am Joaquín* undercuts its own authority over the subject by deferring responsibility. The poem, as well as the epic poet, does describe chicanismo, but that description is neither complete, finished, nor absolutely true. Instead, the descrip-tion of the contemporary Chicano subject points toward an unfin-ished future, toward another time when subjectivity can be more fully realized: "I must choose. . . ." In this way, indefinability complements selection so that chicanismo is presented as an active working out of factors, past, present, and future. The posture of *I am Joaquín* as an unfinished and open text is well situated temporally, both in time, as precursor to other Chicano poetry, and in the times, occurring as it does on the cusp of postmodernism. Although *I am Joaquín* and the Chicano subjectivity it engenders is contemporaneous with the late reading of *Historia de la Nueva Mexico* and an hispano subjectivity, their times are radically different. Consider the retrospective linearity of the hispano as evidenced by some of its subjective markers: early modern linguistic archaisms, early modern religious practice like that of the penitentes, and the valorization of descent from the colonial father. The chicanismo that informs *I am Joaquín* and that it partici-pates in is characterized by different markers: by hybridized language, the Chicano caló; by religious action such as that of the Católicos por la raza, who in the opening chapter of Acosta's *Revolt of the Cockroach People* violently protest Christmas mass by the cardinal in Los Angeles; and by the embracing of mestizaje, conceiving descent from radically disparate sources.

For the most part, the politics of *I am Joaquín* are not particularly radical, despite the poem's place in the Chicano movement. The poem ends, after all, declaring Chicano survival because of very traditional claims to authority: "my blood is pure. / I am Aztec prince and Christian Christ." Even the call to self-author the subject is liberal and concomitant with a humanist drive for social justice. But the refusal "to be absorbed" by U.S. colonialism, with its attendant rejection of the liberal melting pot and the assertion of chicanismo, did inspire a more radical subject. The Chicano movement took its sense of the role of the poet and the function of poetry from the revolutionary and anti-colonial movements of the century. In this way Mexico and Cuba, and Ireland and Algeria, provided the context that granted the popular poet a prime role in the making of the new national subject. Seen in this light, the Chicano poet could define the cultural nationalist subject even if there was little impulse toward a Chicano nation state. Corky Gonzales provided the impetus for a more developed image of the nation in the work of the poet Alurista. In the endeavor to extend the acceptance of chicanismo, Gonzales sponsored the Denver Youth Conference in 1969. There, the participants, mostly through the work of Alurista, put forth the Plan Espiritual de Aztlán, the declaration of cultural autonomy and definition of the Chicano subject and the homeland. The plan and Alurista's own poetic work exceeded the relative liberalism of Gonzales's *I am Joaquín*. It is worth noting that *I am Joaquín* was a bilingual text, that is, English en face with Spanish, whereas Alurista's poetry has always been interlingual, Chicano caló: a very different manifestation of language politics. Alurista's work had profound effects on chicanismo in two ways: he clarified the place of the subject by conceiving Aztlán as the homeland, and he revolutionized the form of Chicano poetry by popularizing interlingual poetry.

Alurista's work and the Chicano subject are born with the advent of postmodernism. But it is the poetry that comes later, when the subject of postmodernism is more fully considered, that works out a most radical subjectivity. His conception of home and his interlingual writing established a matrix for subject formation that would be expanded upon by later writers. Aztlán is an ambiguous home: it is a cultural entity; it is not a state, and it defies the authority of national borders. Interlingualism is an ambiguous mode of expression: it undercuts the authority of any single language; furthermore, it draws into question the very processes of writing and reading by questioning any text's particular selection and combination. Chicano writers who responded to the postmodern turn from modernism were able to draw upon these ambiguities and play out an ambiguous subjectivity.

Time, genre, and hybridity configure the Chicano as an unfinalized subject, one that lacks faith in texts and the relación and yet one that engages in politics. Gloria Anzaldúa and Cherríe Moraga write in an age of the dismantling of heterosexist patriarchies; they write to break apart trenchant rule, order, modes of being. And too, they write to build another subjectivity, not merely alternative but self-consciously critical of its own claims to authority. Central to their project has been the erosion of the rule of genre: Anzaldúa's *Borderlands* and Moraga's *Last Generation* are confused texts generically, replete with poetry, essay, relación, with dream. They are also confused linguistically in the style of the Chicano utterance, playing among and between languages, and rendering any language a matter of choice. *Borderlands* and *Last Generation* articulate hybridity not only in form but in sense as well. Both texts write a hybrid subject by considering first the homeland. *Borderlands* works out spatially, and *Last Generation* temporally, new visions of Aztlán and the place of the Chicano in relation to the United States, to Mexico. The subject they articulate is always implicated in choice, in the tyranny of history, and in the arbitrariness of the hegemony. Anzaldúa and Moraga are simultaneously involved in destroying and building, in iconoclasm and in iconogony. What marks their work is that their building of texts and subjectivity is always self-conscious and not merely ironic; it is dialogic. For them, the subject is forged amid political struggle; and the subjects they help create are always so involved.

And there are those poets who seem to be working in late postmodernism, perhaps even on the post-pomo cusp.[25] Juan Felipe Herrera writes some of the best Chicano poetry today. In a recent conversation I had with the poet Francisco Alarcón, we brought up Herrera's name in discussing the problem of which few Chicano writers are read by mainstream, that is, by Anglo America. Putting aside the matter of talent, Anglo America chooses to print and read those ethnic writers who produce a subjectivity in accord with the hegemony. Alarcón and I agreed that Herrera is an amazing poet whose recognition does not correlate with his talent. Part of that is simple ethnic politics: he is Chicano; he is difficult for monolingual readers. But beyond this, Herrera is a difficult poet, especially difficult for readers who prize a modernist, and even a romantic, ideal. Herrera is the poet of the hybrid subject. For him, each poem is a site of play and conflict, an unfinalized process where the reader must participate.

Generically, his poetry is Chicano, particularly in its form, for even
when the content of a particular poem may not be noticeably Chicano and the language may be English, there is always a dynamic sense
that a sense of self is at stake in the articulation. "In Your Name is X,"
Herrera takes on the hybrid cross of xicanismo and plays out a subjectivity that he repeatedly identifies but ultimately does not define. He
does so, in this instance, in a single language, in simple English, and
yet a simple meaning lies beyond the scope of the poem.

Your Name is X

x the man with the hands trembling
x the unknown echoes of the shadow
x the car flying through the windows
x the woman with bent fantasy jutting
x the falling crates packed with blood
x the romance doubled up against a light
x the suit worn across the sweat electric
x the embrace of night and only night
x the eyes moldering through curtains
x the hair dripping memories
x the nude posing for death
x the neck twisting away from the lips
x the mute performance of sex burning
x the signal that quickens the burial
x the street connecting the final touch
x the blouse stained with confessions
x the room waiting inside the whispers
x the wave flourishing in cages
x the mineral with infinite heat
x the scream fusing through the bone
x the animal leash swollen with tears
x the music caught inside the walls
x the lover biting abstract flesh
x the accident quivering desire
x the poem written and erased forever
x the origin of your name.[26]

And in "Para Siempre Maga," he returns to the X, this time as the sign of a cross between people:

> Al fin estaremos juntos. Ven Amor. Quedaremos escritos en la cumbre de algún precipicio que nadie divisará: uno sobre el otro, como una X mayúscula sobre la tierra del Sur. Brillante. Para siempre.[27]

The post postmodern subject is a xicano subject. X for the Nahuatl of Mexica, mexicano, xicano, and for the chiasmus of a criollo nun. It is a continual coming to be within the exchange of discourses, languages. The xicano is the subject of Aztlán the cultural nation but not the state and not subject to capricious borderlines. It is not a state of being but rather an act, xicando, the progressive tense, ando xicando, actively articulating the self. The infinitive xicar meaning to play, to conflict, to work out dialogically unfinalized versions of self.

Notes

Mestizaje/Difrasismo

1. By Americans I mean people who inhabit the Americas.
2. Garibay defines difrasismo, "Llamo así a un procedimiento que consiste en expresar una misma idea por medio de dos vocablos que se completan en el sentido, ya por ser sinónimos, ya por ser adyacentes." *Llave del Náhuatl* (Mexico: Porrua, 1970), 115.
3. After describing repetition, difrasismo, and parallelism, Garibay concludes, "Todas estas modalidades de expresión se pueden reducir a una fórmula. Es como si el náhuatl no concibiera las cosas sino en forma binaria. Este dualismo de concepción es de los fenómenos más importantes de la lengua, pero su examen más acucioso desborda el ámbito de estas notas" (117).
4. Garibay provides a brief list of diverse difrasismos that illustrate the range of their means of conception. See, for example, page 116.
5. Francisco X. Alarcón, *Snake Poems* (San Francisco: Chronicle Books, 1992); José Montoya, *In Formation: Twenty Years of Joda* (San José: Chusma House, 1992); Lorna Dee Cervantes, *Emplumada* (Pittsburgh: U of Pittsburgh P, 1981); Gloria Anzaldúa, *Borderlands/La Frontera: The New Mestiza* (San Francisco: Spinster/Auntie Lute, 1987).
6. Alurista, *Nationchild Plumaroja* (San Diego: Toltecas en Aztlán, 1972), 3; Gloria Anzaldúa, *Borderlands/La Frontera*, 3; José Antonio Burciaga (San José: Chusma House, 1992).
7. One reason is clearly that the Aztecs represented the dominant political and cultural force in Mexico at the time of the conquest. Nahuatl was the lingua franca in central Mexico and remains spoken by the largest number of people. To put this in perspective, Nahuatl is spoken by about twice as many Indians in Mexico as there are Indians in the United States.
8. For a more thorough discussion of this, see "An Other Tongue."
9. If one could express this as a simple equation, it might be $1+1=3$, not merely that $1+1=1$ and/or $1+1=1$.
10. For more discussion on the U.S. and Mexican nationalist views, see "Beasts and Jagged Strokes of Color" and "An Other Tongue."
11. "El Plan Espiritual de Aztlán," in *Aztlán: Essays on the Chicano Homeland*, ed.

Rudolfo A. Anaya and Francisco Lomeli (Albuquerque: U of New Mexico P, 1989), 1.

12. This reorientation is evident in contemporary Chicano popular culture, in the poster, and the rhetoric of "Who's an immigrant, Pilgrim?" and "We didn't cross the border, the border crossed us."

13. In some ways Gloria Anzaldúa's *Borderlands* expresses essential Indianness as much as does Alurista's "Plan Espiritual de Aztlán," but I argue that the perspective that emphasizes the border between the United States and Mexico is one less focused on Indianness than one that emphasizes a mythical Indian homeland.

14. Of course, the concept of Aztlán as cultural nationalism more closely approaches the concept of the borderlands because it avoids the tendency toward the nation state and instead describes alternate space within the United States.

15. "In Search of Aztlán," in *Aztlán*, 11.

16. "Adulteration and the Nation: Monologic Nationalism and the Colonial Hybrid," in *An Other Tongue: Nation and Ethnicity in the Linguistic Borderlands,* ed. Alfred Arteaga (Durham: Duke U P, 1994), 53.

17. "Myth and Comparative Cultural Nationalism," in *Aztlán,* 114–15.

18. "Franz Fanon and the National Culture of Aztlán," *La Raza* 2.2 (1975), 16–17.

19. *Nationchild Plumaroja*. Alurista addresses his poem in response to Corky Gonzales, the Denver activist and poet who sponsored the 1969 conference and whose poem "I Am Joaquín" is often considered the epic of the Chicano movement.

20. This is of course much more complicated including the nationality Spanish, the various hybrid combinations, American citizenship, and so on.

21. In his letter of March 1, 1974, Alurista accepted the invitation to read at Columbia saying, "i received your carta with great joy as it happens that one of my objectives this año was to visit the thirteen yankee kolonies including New York – I have yet to offer floricanto throughout the eastern seaboard."

Heterotexual Reproduction

1. Octavio Paz goes to great lengths to differentiate Mexican and Chicano subjectivities. In *The Labyrinth of Solitude* (New York: Grove, 1985) he precedes "Sons of La Malinche" with "Pachucos and Other Extremes," that is, he precedes discussion of Mexican genesis with a discussion of Mexicanness at the extreme: the north of the border Chicano. Paz finds the Chicano barely Mexican at all. See "Beasts and Jagged Strokes of Color" for discussion of this.

2. Paz goes into great detail discussing not only the definition but the etymol-

ogy of *chingar*. He traces the word to two Nahuatl words, *chingaste* (lees, residue, sediment) or *xinachtli* (seed). See *Labyrinth of Solitude, 75.*

3. Miscegenation in colonial Latin America is termed generally in Spanish *mestizaje,* and the hybrid offspring is *mestizo;* in French colonial Canada it is *métissage* and *métis*. More specifically, however, mestizo signifies in Spanish the offspring of a Spaniard and an Indian or the offspring that is exactly half Spanish and half Indian. The Spanish colonial project went to great lengths to chart the dissemination of whiteness and to classify races according to the content of miscegenation: there was the mulatto, zambo, sambaigo, lobo, and many more from various combinations of European, African, and American gene pools. Besides reflecting an obvious obsession with classification, the Spanish system reveals a paradigm of race more complex than the simple binary, black and white of Anglo America. It also reserved the possibility that through miscegenation a hybrid could produce monoracially white offspring.

4. Paz is criticized by Chicana feminists for propagating a Mexican narrative that emphasizes Malinche's role in the conquest as the chingada, the mother/traitor, the malinchista. That narrative obfuscates the role of others, the alliance with Tlaxcala, for example, and can very easily lend itself to essentialist sexism. The narrative also demonstrates the alignment of the Mexican national perspective of the Aztec. Briefly, this is further demonstrated in Mexico's rejection of both Cortés and Malinche, the celebration of Cuauhtemoc, and the name of the nation (from Mexica, as the Aztecs called themselves). Chicanos (as does Gloria Anzaldúa, for example) tend to cite Aztec culture when observing the indigenous strain in chicanismo.

5. Latin Americans recognize their racial genesis on día de la raza, the day of the race or people, which in Anglo America is celebrated as Columbus Day. Clearly for both groups, the beginning of colonization is significant, but for Latinos the day is not so much a celebration of the European father (nor the lament of the indigenous mother) as an acknowledgment of the conception of a new race.

6. Another colonial method of eliminating native male is to observe the absence of native masculinity. The colonial project incorporated a feminization of the New World (see "Tricks of Gender Xing"), which not only read the place as feminine but saw the natives of both sexes so. In this way, the colonizer reserves masculinity for the conquistador father.

7. For example see Bartolomé de las Casas, *Devastation of the Indies: A Brief Account* (Baltimore: Johns Hopkins U P, 1992), 82. Tzvetan Todorov dedicates *The Conquest of America* (New York: Harper and Row, 1984) "to the memory of a Mayan woman devoured by dogs." He also quotes Diego de Landa's *Relación de la conquista de Yucatán,* which briefly relates an incident in Montejo's conquest of Yucatán in which a woman was fed to dogs because she insisted on remaining faithful to her Indian husband.

8. Of course this is relative. The Mexican mestizo combines elements of the Spanish and various Indians and is therefore more hybrid than any single people. Yet Spanish subjectivity is hybridized because it composes itself from several European and North African elements. Despite this, the Spaniard is less consciously hybridized than the mestizo for two reasons: (1) mestizo subjectivity includes the Spanish and the Indian, and (2) the Spanish subject conceives itself fundamentally "purer" than the mestizo.

9. Aztlán comprises the Southwestern United States – California, Arizona, New Mexico, Colorado, Utah, Nevada, and Texas. Strictly speaking Texas, having passed an interim decade as a nation, was not directly taken from Mexico by the United States.

10. Bernal Díaz del Castillo commenting that Cortés gave his captains each of the twenty women given him, "Doña Marina, being good-looking, intelligent, and self-assured, went to Alonso Hernández-Puertocarrero, who, as I have already said, was a very grand gentleman, and a cousin of the Count of Medellin. And when Puertocarrero returned to Spain, Doña Marina lived with Cortés, to whom she bore a son named Don Martín Cortés." *The Conquest of New Spain* (London: Penguin, 1963), 82.

11. Not only is his story incomplete, his name is uncertain. Romero observes that Gonzalo is variously given the surnames Guerrero, Marinero, de Morales, and Aroça. It is also possible that there could have been two separate Gonzalos. See "Texts, Pre-Texts, Con-Texts: Gonzalo Guerrero in the Chronicles of Indies," *Revista de Estudios Hispán'cos* 26.3 (1992), 360–1.

12. Bernal Díaz del Castillo quotes Jerónimo de Aguilar's claim that fifteen men and two women shipwrecked in Yucatán. Of the group, only he and Gonzalo Guerrero survived until Cortés arrived (*Conquest of New Spain,* 64). Romero notes that the number varies according to different chroniclers ("Texts," 351).

13. Cortés also had the translation services of two Mayans, Melchor and Julián, who had been captured in an earlier expedition by Francisco Hernández de Córdoba, and in whom Cortés had no trust. Bernal Díaz del Castillo tells how Melchor eventually escaped and joined with the Tabascans, directing them against the Spaniards (*Conquest of New Spain,* 72–4). This is far from the actions of Malinche.

14. Romero quotes a variety of sources that purportedly quote Gonzalo. Here he refers to Bernal Díaz del Castillo ("Texts," 351).

15. Romero observes how Spanish historians condemn Gonzalo Guerrero for being a traitor against Spain, a sinner for marrying an Indian, and even possibly a Jewish convert ("Texts," 353–6).

16. While the female chingón, the chingona, might remain a possibility in Paz's view, Paz remains fixed on a Mexican psychology that emerges from the gendered differentiation of chingón and chingada.

17. And yet there is the great class difference between the two slaves. Of Malinche, Bernal Díaz del Castillo says, "She was a truly great princess, the daughter of *Caciques* and the mistress of vassals, as was very evident in her appearance" and "Doña Marina was a person of great importance, and was obeyed without question by all the Indians of New Spain" (*Conquest of New Spain*, 82, 86). Of Gonzalo Guerrero, he says, "I believe he was a sailor and hailed from Palos" (61).

18. My work here on the subject of heterosexuality, particularly as patriarchal prescript, is indebted to Judith Butler's work on the role of heterosexuality in gender subjectivity. In elaborating upon Monique Wittig's "heterosexual contract" and Adrienne Rich's "compulsory heterosexuality," Butler describes the "heterosexual matrix" as "a hegemonic discursive/epistemic model of gender intelligibility that assumes that for bodies to cohere and make sense there must be a stable sex expressed through a stable gender (masculine expresses male, feminine expresses female) that is oppositionally and hierarchically defined through the compulsory practice of heterosexuality." *Gender Trouble* (New York: Routledge, 1990), 151.

19. I use the term interlingual as distinct from bilingual as suggested by Bruce-Novoa's definition. See "The Other Voice of Silence: Tino Villanueva," in *Modern Chicano Writers,* ed. Joseph Sommers (New York: Prentice Hall, 1979), 133–40. And of course the greater context of linguistic relations I understand as Bakhtinian, beginning with the general, ambient, pervasive heteroglossia that is the fact of humanity. And following Bakhtin, I understand that social forces work toward monologic suppressions of the heteroglot dynamic while others work toward the margins of dialogue and alterity.

20. Actually, the full range of speech acts, the locutionary, illocutionary, perlocutionary, as defined by Paul Ricoeur, *Interpretation Theory* (Fort Worth: Texas Christian U P, 1976), 14. The perlocutionary, in its direct yielding of effect, is the most salient example.

21. "Border of Fear, Border of Desire," *Borderlines Studies in American Culture* 1.1 (1993), 38–69.

Tricks of Gender Xing

1. Such epistemological and representational practices among men regarding women emerge from the sort of male "homosocial" relations, in this case, among European Renaissance male relations, that Eve Kosofsky Sedgwick discusses in *Between Men: English Literature and Male Homosocial Desire* (New York: Columbia U P, 1985). In this essay I consider the European Renaissance masculine homosocial tendency to represent women and New World others in a monologue of the Euro-masculine self. This tendency is homotextual, that is, it is the textualization of homosocial representational practice.

2. Note, for example, in chapters 157 and 158 of *Las Sergas de Esplandián,* "Sabed que á la diestra mano de las Indias hubo una isla, llamada California, muy llegada á la parte del Paríso Terrenal, la cual fué poblada de mujeres negras, sin que algun varon entre ellas hubíese, que casi como las amazonas era su estilo de vivir," and "[L]a reina Califia salida de la mar, armada ella y sus mujeres de aquellas armas de oro, sembradas todas de piedras muy preciosas, que en la su ínsula California como las piedras del campo se hallaban." *Libros de Caballerias* 40 (Madrid, 1963), 593, 540.

3. My understanding of the process and institution of "patriarchy" is indebted to Gerda Lerner, *The Creation of Patriarchy* (New York: Oxford U P, 1986). As for "masculist," Gayatri Chakravorty Spivak's opposition of public "masculist" space and private "feminist" space inspires my use of the term and the spatialization of tropes. See "Explanation and Culture: Marginalia," in *In Other Worlds* (New York: Methuen, 1988), 103–17.

4. The *differences* in the style of tropics in the Spanish *musa décima* and that in the English tenth muse points to greater differences in style in the Spanish and English representations of the Old/New World relations. While the Spanish and English similarly used the New World woman writer as a spatial and temporal linking point, they differed in the representation of their countries' relationships with America, as well as those with classical Europe. A contrast of the title pages demonstrates the different ways in which articulation of a "tenth muse" draws a line of cultural authority from classical Europe, through either Spain or England, to the New World.

   The first tenth muse was the English, Anne Bradstreet's *The Tenth Muse lately sprung up in America. or Severall Poems* (London, 1650). The trope did not appear on either of the two subsequent and American editions; they were simply entitled *Several Poems* (Boston, 1678 and 1758). Sor Juana's *Inundación Castálida de la única poetisa, musa dézima* (Madrid, 1689) was published in nine Spanish editions, from 1689 to 1725, in Madrid, Barcelona, Zaragoza, and Valencia. After the first printing *Inundación Castálida* was changed to *Poemas,* but "tenth muse" remained throughout. And in the posthumous collection, *Fama, Y Obras Posthumas del Fénix de México, Décima Musa, Poestisa Americana* (Madrid, 1700), she was not only Tenth Muse, but Phoenix of Mexico and Female American Poet.

   Over the course of Bradstreet's title pages, "tenth muse" did not persist and a reference to Rome was put at greater remove. The London edition stated, *Together with an Extract Epitomie of the Four Monarchies, viz. The Assyrian, Persian, Grecian, Roman;* that is, Rome was included as the latest of the Old World empires. The Boston editions, however, clearly truncate Roman presence, altering the "Roman" of the first edition to *And beginning of the Romane Common-wealth, to the end of their last King* (1678) and to *Roman Common Wealth, from its beginning to the End of their last King* (1758). Sor

Juana's title pages brim with Roman Catholicism. Sor Juana is the *Religiosa Professa en el Monasterio de San Geronimo de la Imperial Ciudad,* religion and empire simultaneously defining her in a single line.

5. It is worth noting that both New World muses were Euro-Americans. Anne Bradstreet was born in England and immigrated to America as a child. Sor Juana was a criolla, that is, one born in America of nonracially mixed, European lineage. Neither was, even in part, racially native to the New World.

6. And yet, while Sor Juana's texts cross the masculist canon, they do so canonically. Howard Mancing notes the extreme degree to which Sor Juana is recognized as part of the canon, for not only is she anthologized at rates comparable to the Siglo de oro poets, but her poem "Hombres necios" is the fourth most anthologized of any Spanish poem. See "A Consensus Canon of Hispanic Poetry," *Hispania* 69.1 (1986), 53–81. Also, in its entry on Spanish American Poetry, the *Princeton Encyclopedia of Poetry and Poetics* includes a single example, one of Sor Juana's sonnets, "which the critics compared to those of Lope de Vega and Shakespeare." In contrast, Anne Bradstreet seems to rank much less often among the famous and dead white men of English letters.

7. The early date of Sor Juana's textual representation of a slave speaking Afro-Spanish can be appreciated when compared to the date of the earliest visual representation of a slave in Anglo art. The first recorded representation is George Morland's "The Slave Trade," shown in 1788, more than a century after Sor Juana's villancicos. See Richard Dorment, *Times Literary Supplement,* September 15–21, 1989.

Yet musically, there were analogs of Afro-Spanish and Nahuatl-Spanish compositions in colonial Mexico. Two composers were Sor Juana's contemporaries, Antonio de Salazar (Spain, 1650–Mexico, 1715) and her predecessor, Gaspar Fernandez (Portugal, 1578–Mexico, 1629). Salazar's "Tarara, tarara," very similar to Sor Juana's Afro-Spanish writing, begins, "Tarara tarara qui yo soy Anton / ninglito di nacimiento / qui lo canto lo mas y mijo." Fernandez wrote both in Afro-Spanish and Nahuatl-Spanish. His "Dame albriçia" begins, "Dame albriçia mano Anton / que Jisu naçe en Guînea. / Una lunçuya y viejo su pagre son / yebamo le culaçion," and the complete text of his "Xicochi xicochi conetzintle" is "Xicochi, xicochi, conetzintle / caomiz hui hui joco / in angelos me, / alleluya."

8. My reference to Sor Juana as a protofeminist follows the qualified sense of "feminist" suggested by the Grupo Feminista de Cultura, "Si por feminista entendemos a una mujer que ha tomado conciencia de su opresión como mujer y trata de influir de algún modo para transformar esta realidad, podemos decir que Juana es feminista, en la medida en que podía serlo una mujer sola, en la segunda mitad del siglo XVII." *Respuesta a Sor Filotéa de la Cruz* (Barcelona: Laertes, 1979), 19.

9. I borrow the notion of "tricks" from Josefina Ludmer's analysis of the rhetorical strategy of the *Respuesta*, in "Las tretas del débil," in *La sartén por el mango*, ed. Patricia Elena González and Eliana Ortega (Río Piedras: Ediciones Huracan, 1985), 47–54. For Ludmer, Sor Juana's *Respuesta* is an example of the rhetoric and tactics employed by weaker voices, in this case, the feminist voice in the masculist context. Ludmer focuses upon the use of "to know," "to say," and "no" in Sor Juana's dialogue with the Bishop of Puebla. Sor Juana's use of those words and her posture as a woman writer are manifested in the "tricks of the weak." Also, the rhetoric of the trick, its chiasmus, is suggested in Sedgwick's *Between Men*, 15.

10. Groupe μ identifies four tropes that operate similarly; they differ in the area upon which they operate. They are chiasmus (which operates on syntax), metonymy (on semantics), neologism/archaism (on morphology), and allegory (on logic). See *Rhétorique Générale* (Paris: Editions du Seuil, 1982), 49.

11. "Hegemony" here is to be understood as generally defined by Raymond Williams in "Hegemony," in *Marxism and Literature* (Oxford: Oxford U P, 1977), 108–14 and as more specifically defined in the colonial context by Abdul JanMohamad in "The Economy of Manichean Allegory: The Economy of Racial Difference in Colonial Literature," in *"Race," Writing, and Difference*, ed. Henry Louis Gates, Jr. (Chicago: U of Chicago P, 1986), 78–106. The distinction between "strategies" and "tactics," I borrow from Michel de Certeau, *The Practice of Everyday Life* (Berkeley and Los Angeles: U of California P, 1984), and from Louie Montrose, "The Work of Gender in the Discourse of Discovery," *Representations* 33 (1991), 1–41. "Tricks," as feminist tactic, is from Josefina Ludmer; see note 9 above.

12. See *Respuesta*, 19. In the introduction to the English translation, Margaret Sayers Peden calls the *Respuesta* "a defense of the rights of women to education and culture that was to find no equal – in America or in Europe – for at least a century and a half" (*A Woman of Genius* [Salisbury: Lime Rock, 1982], 4). It would be worthwhile to contrast the uses of Sor Juana by the contemporaries, hers and mine, who name her "musa décima" and "primera feminista de américa."

13. Yet, as Emilie Bergmann reminds me, the matter of ceasing writing after the *Respuesta* is complicated by the possibility of an earlier letter of response. In the English version of *Sor Juana o las trampas de la fé*, published as *Sor Juana* (Cambridge: Harvard U P, 1988), Octavio Paz reprints a letter attributed to Sor Juana that defends her writing very much in the manner of the *Respuesta* but is assumed to have been written a decade earlier, in 1681 or 1682. The *Autodefensa espiritual de Sor Juana*, discovered and printed by Aurelio Tapia Méndez (Monterrey, 1981), would seem to make the *Respuesta* Sor Juana's second of two defenses, after the first of which she continued writing for another decade. The authenticity of the *Autodefensa* is questionable, how-

ever, because the manuscript is neither in Sor Juana's hand nor likely copied during her lifetime.

14. In fact I simplify by avoiding Octavio Paz's conjecture in *Sor Juana o las trampas de la fé* (Barcelona: Seix Barral, 1982) that Bishop Manuel of Puebla was both friend and champion of Sor Juana and published *Carta Athenagorica* in an effort to attack a particularly misogynist competitor for the bishopric of Mexico City. "Tricks of Gender Xing" focuses on text and rhetoric, on the discursive relations between Sor Juana and a prefabricated Euro-male homosocial world view.

15. The *Carta Athenagorica* (Puebla, 1690) begins by addressing the anonymous authority: "Muy señor mio. De las bacherillerias de una conversación, que en la merçed que Umd. el deseo de ver por escrito algunos discursos que alli hize de repente sobre los Sermones de un exçelente Orador . . . le obedezco en lo mas dificil" (9).

16. The translation is mine. This is excerpted from the introductory letter of "Sor Filotéa" addressed to Sor Juana in *Carta Athenagorica*, 2–7.

17. In the fourth volume of Méndez Plancarte's *Obras Completas de Sor Juana Inés de la Cruz, Comedias, Sainetes Y Prosa* (Mexico, 1952), Alberto Salceda explains the title "Carta Athenagorica": "*Tit. – Atenagórica:* digna de la sabiduría de Minerva: 'de las voces griegas *Athena,* Minerva, y *agora,* arenga, y de sufijo *ica,* que vale tanto como propio de, digno de,' explica don Ezequiel A. Chávez" (*Ensay. de psicologia,* 300), 631. Of course quite another reading is made possible if "Athenagorica" is read in reference to "Athenagorus." This more logically correct entymology is argued for in the recent work of Amy Williamsen; see "Imposed Titles and Interpretation in Sor Juana and Maria de Zayas," forthcoming in *Revista de Estudios Hispánicos.*

18. But of course, her feminine and American body always renders somewhat ironic any articulation of a Euro-male homosocial discourse. "Woman" and "American" function as heterosocial and heterotextual markers.

19. Very similar to "San Pedro Nolasco" are "Asunción" (1676), which also features Pilico and an unnamed Nahuatl-speaking Indian, and "San José" (1690), which features Negro and Indio. There are some seven villancicos entitled "Asunción" written by Sor Juana. The "Asunción" I refer to in this essay is dated differently by Alfonso Méndez Plancarte, *Obras Completas de Sor Juana Inés de la Cruz* and by Georgina Sabat de Rivers, *Inundación Castálida* (Madrid: Castalia, 1982). I use Méndez Plancarte's date, but I am indebted to Georgina Sabat de Rivers for reading this chapter and for providing valuable criticism.

20. There are other readings made possible by the chiasmus. The subject for *era,* for example, can just as easily be "I," "She," or "It" as it is "He." Then there is *como,* which also translates as "I eat." This allows the reading of *como cura* as "I eat; he cures" and "I eat (a/the) priest."

21. In describing sixteenth-century ensaladas of Matheo Flecha the Elder, Carmen Gomez notes the characteristic mixing of the genre, "Dans son *Arte Poética Española* (Salamanque, 1592), Juan Diaz Rengifo définit l'*Ensalada* comme «une composition de strophes de quatre vers dans lesquels se mêlent toutes sortes de mètres, non seulement espagnols mais provenant aussi d'autres langues, sans order des uns aux autres, au gré du poète; et selon la variété des paroles, on change la musique.»" *Ensaladas,* Hespèrion 20, Astrée Auvidis E7742, 1987, 3.

22. The tocotín is a Mexican form of word, music, and dance. Sor Juana's version in "San Pedro Nolasco" is interlingual; she introduces it as "un tocotín mestizo de Español y Mejicano."

23. Pilico's style of interlingualism is heterophonic; the Indian's is specifically heteroglot. This follows Bakhtin's distinctions of dialogism within a national language and that between national languages. See Todorov, *Mikhail Bakhtin: The Dialogical Principle* (Minneapolis: U of Minnesota P, 1984), 56-9.

24. Sor Juana's relative orientation toward Europe or Mexico is a point of contention for those who comment on her work. Octavio Paz emphasizes her cosmopolitanism, her complete Eurocentricism, and gives as illustration her poem "El Sueño." See *Children of the Mire* (Cambridge: Harvard U P, 1974), 138. Luis Leal, on the other hand, focuses on the villancicos and emphasizes her facility with the popular speech of Mexico in "El 'Tocotín Mestizo' de Sor Juana," *Abside* 18.1 (1954), 51–64.

An Other Tongue

1. I am, of course, speaking of relative differences. But it is worth contrasting Eliot's "The Waste Land" with Burciaga's "Poema en tres idiomas y caló" (the complete text of Burciaga's poem is appended to the end of this essay). Clearly the styles of their multilingual poems differ sharply, and it is worthwhile to ask of these poems what discourses come into dialogue and who are the participants in dialogue.

2. Bruce-Novoa noted the qualitative differences in the styles of multilingualism in his seminal contrasting of "bilingualism" and "interlingualism" in "The Other Voice of Silence: Tino Villanueva," in *Modern Chicano Writers,* 133–40.

3. I wrote these words on January 12, 1990, the day that "Border Patrol's School Raid Outrages Officials" (Kimura A3) appeared in the *Santa Cruz Sentinel.* In addition, there was another "chicano" article four pages later, "Has Law Led to Discrimination?" (Bishop A7), which begins, "A state panel has concluded that the 1986 immigration law has resulted in widespread job discrimination against Hispanic residents and others." It, too, strikes me as dramatically ironic.

4. Of course, other languages are also suppressed. Language marginalization can be accorded by degree of dissimilarity, linguistic Anglos valuing more highly German than Vietnamese, for example, and by a variety of other factors of perceived worth. French or Latin can be valued more highly than Yiddish or Gaelic for reasons of imagined cultural purity, aesthetics, or antecedence.

5. The distinction between "making an identity" and "making a space" can be considered to be the difference in conceiving subjectification either as a metaphoric or a metonymic relation of discursive elements. The perception of subjectification as the creation of identity, if "creation" is seen as a choice from potential identities, would emphasize selection and paradigm. Finding a space, as the border, for example, would seem relatively more dependent on spatial context, on contiguity, and on syntagma.

6. As Bakhtin says, "The world of poetry, no matter how many contradictions and insoluble conflicts the poet develops within it, is always illumined by one unitary and indisputable discourse. Contradictions, conflicts, and doubts remain in the object, in thoughts, in living experiences – in short, in the subject matter – but they do not enter into the language itself" (*Dialogic Imagination* [Austin: U of Texas P, 1981], 286). And yet this is qualified. Todorov observes that in his later writing, Bakhtin blurs the absolute distinction between the genres, "Should poetry attempt to avail itself of this resource [multiple voices], it is immediately drawn to the side of the novel. Bakhtin constantly cites Pushkin's *Eugene Onegin* as an example of the novel, not of poetry" (*Mikhail Bakhtin: The Dialogical Principle*, 64).

7. I take up this issue at greater length in "Tricks of Gender Xing," where I examine the gender and racial politics of the imperial Spanish telos and how its narrative line is "crossed" by Sor Juana Inés de la Cruz in colonial Mexico.

8. There are other ways to consider the differences of these multilingual styles. One is to recall Bruce-Novoa's distinction between bilingualism and interlingualism so as to contrast Eliot and Pound's *alternation* of languages with Montoya and Burciaga's *hybridization*. Another way is to bring into consideration the border. Eliot and Pound were willing immigrants to countries they felt to be seminal to the course of Western civilization. That Eliot became "more British than the British" and Pound preached Mussolini propaganda demonstrate a marked degree of assimilation. For Montoya and Burciaga, and Chicanos in general, the border is not so much a line to cross en route to becoming another as a zone where one lives and has to struggle to articulate an intercultural self. Following this differentiation, it is interesting to look at two essays by Tzvetan Todorov and Ada Savin in *An Other Tongue*. Savin addresses Todorov's "Dialogism and Schizophrenia" in her "Bilingualism and Dialogism: Another Reading of Lorna Dee Cervantes's Poetry," arguing that there is a great distinction between the "chosen" bilingualism of the willing immigrant and the "obligatory" bilingualism of the nonimmigrant minority.

9. Clearly, the colonial relationship requires an extreme exercise of power, yet there are other relationships that require a tremendous amount of power; class and gender relationships are two obvious examples. Exhaustive and continual discursive activity is required to establish and maintain those relationships and the unequal distributions of power that structure them. In addition, the marginalization of those at the extremes of the human age range and those with low mental or physical capabilities requires huge expenditures of energy. Then, too, the expenditures of energy in maintaining the psychology, for example, of "superiority" are significant.

10. The seminal text is Robert Blauer's *Racial Oppression in America* (New York: Harper, 1972). Chicano historians who employ the internal colonial model include Rodolfo Acuña, *Occupied America* (New York: Harper, 1981) and Mario Barrera, *Race and Class in the Southwest* (Notre Dame: Notre Dame U P, 1979). In *Internal Colonialism: The Celtic Fringe in British National Development, 1536–1966* (Berkeley: U of California P, 1975), Michael Hechter cites the popularization of the term "internal colonialism" among U.S. black nationalists in the 1960s but traces its earlier use by Lenin in *The Development of Capitalism in Russia* and by Gramsci in "The Southern Question."

11. Compared to Indians and Chicanos, Afro-American blacks are linguistically more autocolonized: they speak English; they are the most "Americanized"; their cultural production is the most integrated into Anglo-American culture. And yet, they remain extremely marginalized. While the former slaves may have assimilated the master's language, they have reworked it in the process. By rewriting Standard American English, black English dehegemonizes it.

12. A very good discussion of this is Sander L. Gilman's "Black Bodies, White Bodies: Toward an Iconography of Female Sexuality in Late Nineteenth-Century Art, Medicine, and Literature," in *"Race," Writing, and Difference,* 223–61. Noteworthy is the reliance of scientific discourse on synecdoche: one part of the black female anatomy signaled the essential difference of the black race; the size of Sarah Bartmann's buttocks "proved" the subhumanity of all blacks. And still today, the physical artifact, that is, the scientific "proof," the dismembered flesh of the most famous raceme, Sarah Bartmann's buttocks and genitals, remain on display for scientific study in the aptly named Museé de l'homme in Paris.

13. The enumeration and distribution of Chicanos is currently a hot topic in U.S. law. The census question of counting "illegals" embraces several concerns: the definition of "illegal" (read Mexican), the relative value (does one illegal equal one legal?), the significance of as accurate a count of illegals as for legals. States like Texas and California demand that illegals be counted. Cities like New York and Los Angeles demand accuracy so that none be missed. At the same time, Los Angeles is being sued for gerrymandering district lines to

restrict Chicano representation in the city council. These points illustrate the borders that exist north of the border.

"Legal" language, that is, language use permitted by law, remains a major concern for Chicanos. Corporal punishment has been regularly employed throughout the Southwest for the speaking of Spanish in public schools. The beating of children has recently been outlawed in California but remains appropriate behavior in Texas. On the other hand, it is currently illegal in California and Florida, for example, to speak any language other than English while on the job at certain workplaces.

14. Art cultivates racism in two related ways: first, artistic discourse denies the other presence and second, to the limited extent that is does represent the other, it denigrates. Art as racist representation is the subject of two contemporary reviews. Richard Dorment considers black absence in *Times Literary Supplement* (September 15–21, 1989):

> Can it really be true that the earliest recorded painting to deal with the subject of slavery was painted as late as 1788, the year George Morland exhibited "The Slave Trade" at the Royal Academy? Like so many questions raised by *Slaves and Liberators,* the first part of Hugh Honour's two-volume study *The Image of the Black in Western Art,* the answer demonstrates the impossibility of ever separating art from its social and historical background. For until the subject of slavery and its abolition existed as a social question, it could not exist as a subject for the arts – even (surprisingly) in paintings illustrating the lives and legends of the saints. And right from the beginning, from the moment when Morland broached the theme, art mirrored all the evasions, stereotypes, velleities, and falsifications that permitted the institution to continue in the West.

Several points are worth considering. One is the absence of slavery in artistic discourse and from artistic representation. Another is the converse of Morland's declaration of the dependency of the artistic subject on the social subject, that is, perhaps the social question of slavery could not exist until the artistic subject did. Then again, perhaps the two are interdependent. Finally, the observation that art mirrors social reality indicates the extent to which art tropes itself as the mirror of the world.

Michael Kemmelman observes in the *New York Times* (January 18, 1990):

> "Facing History: The Black Image in American Art, 1710–1940" is an exhibition that no thinking person can walk through without feeling a measure of both sorrow and anger. The 100 or so paintings, sculptures and drawings gathered at the Corcoran Gallery of Art testify to a racism so ingrained in the American consciousness that artists – the overwhelming number of them white, but some of whom were black – thought nothing

about stereotyping blacks as "grotesque buffoons, servile menials, comic entertainers or threatening subhumans," writes Guy C. McElroy, the show's curator, in the exhibition catalogue.

He continues, "It is the casualness of the cruelty that leaves the deepest impression on the viewer. Sometimes the methods of expression are sophisticated, the prejudices subtly masked." Perhaps most sorrowful is the participation of black artists in the casual cruelty.

15. The troping differs from context to context and is related to the quality and intensity of the monologism. But clearly, common to the various antitheses is the simple statement: self is what other is not. The self has the positive characteristics the other lacks. The other has the negative characteristics the self lacks. A double negative definition: the self is the negative of the negative other.

In "Forms of Wildness" and "The Noble Savage Theme as Fetish," Hayden White demonstrates the necessary definition of self that accompanies the antithetical troping of the other, European troping of indigenous Americans as "noble savages" differentiates them from Europeans and stresses their homogeneity. It simultaneously tropes the European upper class as "savage nobles," thereby increasing difference within "European," enhancing its heterogeneity. *Tropics of Discourse* (Baltimore: Johns Hopkins U P, 1978), 150–82, 183–96.

16. For discussion of the monologic impulse of nationalism and the single-mindedness of the narratives of nation, see "Beasts and Jagged Strokes of Color."

17. It is worthwhile here to consider the Yaqui, whose territory straddles the Arizona/Sonora border, whose immigration situation is somewhat analogous to the Chicano's, but who have a history of repression by mestizo Mexicans.

18. There is a little gradation of relative Indian worth. For example, when Anglo-Americans claim to have "Indian blood," it is most often claimed to be Cherokee, in great part, I believe, because Cherokees are perceived to be the noblest savages. In this regard, see Vine Deloria, *Custer Died for Your Sins* (New York: Avon, 1969), 3. Further, it is not mere coincidence that Cherokees more fully assimilated English and learned Western writing sooner than other Indians did.

19. Considering that Colonial American slavery was based on an essential subhumanity, at least partially demonstrated by absolute illiteracy, imagine what it must have meant to have to acknowledge that a slave girl could write and was publishing poetry in English. Phillis Wheatley's writing and its confirmation by the likes of John Hancock forced a reconsideration of the rhetoric and began the arduous rewriting of "black."

20. This is, of course, on the level of national consciousness and on the level of

the individual for the majority of Americans who imagine themselves living far from reservations and centers of Indian population. Overt racism still thrives at the junctures of Anglo and Indian cultures; there the living "injun" is very much present.

21. This etymology can be metaphoric rather than literal as in cowboy/*vaquero* and other instances of English occurrence before American contact with Texas Mexicans. Yet even in those cases, it is clear that the cowboy usage is shaped by the metaphoric Spanish/Mexican/Chicano accent.

22. This is why archival work like that of Luis Torres is so significant for both Chicano and "American" literary histories. Torres has recovered a wealth of literature written by Chicanos and successfully demystifies the impression of illiteracy; see his "Bilingualism as Satire in Nineteenth-Century Chicano Poetry," in *An Other Tongue* and *The World of Early Chicano Poetry, 1848–1910* (Encino: Floricanto, 1993).

23. Beth Haas observes that during the Spanish conquest of California, the descendants of Europeans were described as "gente de razón," while the Indians were "gente sin razón." See *Conquest and Historical Identities in California, 1769–1936* (Berkeley and Los Angeles: U of California P, 1995), 31–2.

24. Among Chicanos it is observed that after Texan Chicanos said "mi casa es su casa," the gringo replied, "go back to Mexico."

25. That such a juxtaposition, a dialogism, of alternate subjectifications begins with literary writing is not insignificant. In "French Feminism in an International Frame," Gayatri Chakravorty Spivak observed of feminist rewriting of dominant culture, quoting Catherine Clément, "One would cut through all the heavy layers of ideology that have borne down since the beginnings of the family and private property: that can be done only in the imagination. And that is precisely what feminist action is all about: to change the imaginary in order to be able to act on the real, to change the very forms of language which by its structure and history has been subject to a law that is patrilinear, therefore masculine" (*In Other Worlds,* 145). It is in the realm of imaginary writing that relationships other than those authoritatively prescribed come to be. This rewriting can begin with deconstruction. See Spivak's "Bonding in Difference," in *An Other Tongue*.

26. José Antonio Burciaga, *Undocumented Love,* 39–41.

Beasts and Jagged Strokes of Color

1. *Exiles of Desire* (Houston, 1985).

2. That this seems loose Bakhtin, I am aware. I argue that when compared to the narrative of nation, hybridized poetry is relatively more dialogic. And while the scope of this essay is Chicano heteroglot *poetry,* it could just as well have considered Chicano heteroglot drama.

3. My understanding of the imagination of nation is informed by discussions with Maria Koundoura and by reading a draft of "Multinationalism: Redrawing the Map of the Intellectual's Labor in the Age of Post Coloniality," Phd. diss., Stanford U, 1993.

4. It should be noted that American English and Mexican Spanish are colonial languages and that the United States and Mexico therefore lack the metonymic link of language and land and identity that England and Spain have. In England or Spain one speaks and *is* English or Spanish. I believe that this is a reason why both countries still have royalty: the metonymies of language, space, and nation are enhanced by the contiguity of the ideal national bloodline. The United States and Mexico differ in their distances from the English and Spanish imaginations. The name "U.S.A." is perhaps less denominational than descriptive and creates the problem of an unclear nationality (American is, after all, a continental identification). The ideal Mexican national is not racially equivalent to the Spaniard; Mexicans are racial hybrids, mestizos.

5. The question can be asked, how thick is thick? In "Border Matters: Sites of Cultural Crossing," José Saldívar answers: the borderlands stretch "from shanty barrios of Tijuana/San Diego to the rich surf and turf of Santa Barbara" (forthcoming in *Borders and Diaspora,* ed. James Clifford and José Saldívar).

6. There are, of course, many others who must relate to nations that circumscribe or incise them. Each borderland, each material site of conflict, be it home to Basque, Gypsy, Maori, Palestinian, Quebecois, or Yaqui (to name but a few), constitutes a particular set of relations with particular conflicts offering particular options for survival.

7. Such discursive interplay undermines the authority of the absolutely differentiating borderline. It is the place of heteroglossia where English and Spanish and other national languages compete for authority and for presence, and the place of heterophony where various intralingual discourses compete as well. The complex heteroglossia of the zone is simplified here for brevity only. But as example, Chicano poetry can be heteroglot by putting Spanish, English, and Nahuatl in dialogue, and it can be heterophonic by putting conflicting class discourses in dialogue.

8. It should be noted that under such dialogic conditions, definitions themselves remain pliable and less fixed than in a more rigid discursive relationship. So it is easy to imagine the coming to be of *chicano* as syncope of the present participle *chicando* from the intransitive *chicar,* or perhaps, *chicanar.* That verb arises beside *chingar,* which Octavio Paz sees as the definitive verb of Mexican identity, as in the Mexican nationalist cry "¡Que viva México, hijos de la chingada!" Both derive from the Nahuatl: chicano from

mexica (Mexican, Aztec); chingar from *chingaste* (lees, residue, sediment) or *xinachtli* (seed). See *Labyrinth of Solitude*, 75. Both verbs construe subjectivity as an act, but while Mexicans defer that act to the primal act between chingón and chingada, Mexicans are, after all, *hijos de la chingada,* Chicanos instead locate subject formation in the present act of individually identifying as part of the collective chicanada. Two final points, one literary, the other orthographic. Play in the Mexican etymologies and phonetic similarities colors the interpretation of a poem by Lorna Cervantes, where Mexico can call the Chicana a "bland pochaseed," a chingada chicana. See "Oaxaca, 1974," *Emplumada.* Chicano politics today often makes an anticolonial stand orthographically, so that *Chicano* is presented *Xicano,* more native, less colonized, and declaring our active and quotidian crossings. Following this, *xicar* and *xicanar,* the imperatives, prescribe an imperative of action: los xicanos son porque xican (o xicanan). The self exists in an act. See "Late Epic, Post Postmodern."

9. "Pachuco and Other Extremes," *Labyrinth of Solitude*, 9–28.
10. Pachuco is an older term for urban Chicano youth and is marked by cultural and linguistic hybridization. It is generally acknowledged that pachuco consciousness is the forerunner of contemporary Chicano consciousness.
11. *Nationchild Plumaroja.* "Pachuco Paz" is on page Serpiente 24; the book follows a Mesoamerican base-five numeration.
12. A problem in conceiving a double-voicedness that is cast by irony is that irony can be understood as a poetic trope, which for Bakhtin would signal single-voicedness. It has been pointed out to me that the intermediary relating double-voicedness and irony is parody and that in "Discourse in the Novel," Bakhtin exemplifies double-voicedness by the use of parody in *Little Dorrit.* Dickens's parodic stylization strikes me as similar to Alurista's ironic rearticulation.
13. The placa, which Paz is likely to have come across in Los Angeles, would have been literally indecipherable for him. In the first place, it would have been written in stylized Chicano script unfamiliar to him, and secondly, meaning would have eluded him. For example, a placa such as "Chuy, L'il Oso HMV R c/s XIV putos" could be translated as "The emblem, 'Jesus and Little Bear from the superior neighborhood, Lower Maravilla, Los Angeles,' is immune from deprecation and deprecates Northern Californians."
14. *An Other Tongue*, 113–23.
15. For Nancy, the mestizo is not only the hybrid of races and of cultures but the hybrid of time as well. In a continual coming-to-be, the mestizo has either no present or has a present hybridized with the past and the future. The nonmestizo, the racially and culturally finalized subject, is fixed in the present and is monochronic.

16. As I write this, my university is on strike, and I am reminded of an alternate meaning of "scab." The strikebreaker "scab" works to finalize labor relations that strikers actively wound.

17. This is from the introduction, page 3. See note 11 above regarding pagination.

18. "Poem for the Young White Man Who Asked Me How I, an Intelligent, Well-Read Person Could Believe in the War Between Races," *Emplumada*, 35.

19. Houston, 1991.

20. Translation, a difficult task at best, is more difficult with the interlingual text. "México gags, ¡Esputa! / on this bland pochaseed" can be translated as "Mexico gags, she's a whore, on this bland Mexican American seed." "Esputa" recalls "escupa" (spit), and "seed" can be read in light of Octavio Paz's discussion of "chingar." See note 8 above.

21. That the hybrid verbal expression is heard as song is significant. For Bakhtin the multivoiced text was described in musical terms, it was polyphonic. In his definition of Bakhtin's "orchestration," Michael Holquist explains that polyphony is achieved through orchestration and that "In oral/aural arts, the 'overtones' of a communicative act individualize it . . . . The possibilities of orchestration make any segment of text almost infinitely variable"; see *The Dialogic Imagination*, 431. It is significant that Chicano hybridized poetics contrasts difficulty with "words" with utter fluency in singing.

Blood Points

1. *Cuentos Chicanos: A Short Story Anthology,* ed. Rudolfo Anaya and Antonio Márquez (Albuquerque: U of New Mexico P, 1984).

2. In the transition from publication in *Cuentos Chicanos* to that in *Last of the Menu Girls,* "Willow Game" lost the "Today" of that sentence. Its absence in the Arte Publico version affects the reading of the story and is, according to the author, an error. That absence prevents the clear understanding that (1) the second attack took place on the same day that the narrator tells the story, and that (2) the point of the story is the explanation of "today" by virtue of past events. Denise Chávez, *Last of the Menu Girls* (Houston: Arte Publico, 1986), 50.

3. Oscar Zeta Acosta, *The Autobiography of a Brown Buffalo* (San Francisco: Straight Arrow, 1972) and *The Revolt of the Cockroach People* (San Francisco: Straight Arrow, 1973).

4. Charley Trujillo, *Soldados: Chicanos in Viet Nam* (San José: Chusma House, 1990) and *Dogs from Illusion* (San José: Chusma House, 1994).

5. Francisco X. Alarcón, *No Golden Gate for Us* (Santa Fe: Pennywhistle, 1993), 17.

Late Epic, Post Postmodern

1. Of course the problem of time is not so easily dismissed; I do so here to pursue an argument subject to the order of literature and history as founded upon Western notions of time. I take up the problems of time, including the question of the reality of its existence, in a lengthier study, "Lacuna."

2. For example, the basic principle of definition is the same whether the genre be "epic" or "novel" or "tragedy" or "pulp fiction." But this does not mean that any genre is as fully defined nor as rigidly defined as any other.

3. See *Speech Genres* (Austin: U of Texas P, 1986) for Bakhtin's writing from the 1970s.

4. Clearly *La Historia de la Nueva Mexico* locates itself after, and in a progression from, the *Aeneid*. Two other works that do so similarly are Ariosto's *Orlando Furioso* (1516) and Tasso's *Gerusalemme liberata* (1579). Ariosto (1474–1532) was a contemporary of Hernán Cortés; Tasso (1544–95), a contemporary of Villagrá.

> Le donne, i cavillier, l'arme, gli amori
> le cortesie, l'audaci imprese io canto,
> che furo al tempo che passaro i Mori
> d'Africa il mare, e in Francia nocquer tanto,
> seqendo l'ire e i giovenil furori
> d'Agramante lor re, che si diè vanto
> de vendicar la morte di Troiano
> sopre re Carlo imperator romano.
>
> (Ariosto, *Orlando Furioso,* Canto primo, 1–8)

> Canto l'arme pietose e 'l capitano
> che 'l gran sepolcro liberò di Cristo.
> Molto egli oprò co 'l senno e con la mano,
> molto soffrì nel glorioso acquisto;
> e in van l'Inferno vi s'oppose, e in vano
> s'armò d'Asia e di Libia il popol misto.
> Il Ciel gli diè favore, e sotto a i santi
> segni ridusse i suoi compagni erranti.
>
> (Tasso, *Gerusalemme liberata,* Libro primo, 1–8)

5. See "Tricks of Gender Xing" for discussion of Cortés, *Las Sergas de Esplandián* and the naming of California. In 1492 Nebrija published a grammar and a dictionary of Castilian, the first of a modern European language. In the introduction to the dictionary he asserts the role of language in the making of empire. See Alfred Arteaga, *First Words: Origins of the European Nation,* Working Paper 3.17, Center for German and European Studies, University of California, 1994.

6. And the impact on Europe was written in Spanish. The first news of the New World, Columbus's letter to the king, was written in Spanish, then translated into Latin for broader European dissemination. It is indicative of the linguistic state of Europe that when Spain embarked on empire, the lingua franca was still Latin.

7. "The received idea is that the Hispanic imperial text failed partly because, again over-simplifying, the conjuncture between conquest and mode of production was not yet right. Britain with its industrial revolution was the one that could launch full-fledged capitalist imperialism." See "Bonding in Difference, Interview with Alfred Arteaga," in *The Spivak Reader,* ed. Donna Landry and Gerald MacLean (New York: Routledge, 1996), 23.

8. In the first century of empire, native populations were eliminated entirely in places like Cuba; in Mexico, the population dropped 95 percent, from 20 million inhabitants to 1 million.

9. Chronologically and geographically between New Mexico's *Historia* of 1610 and Chile's *Araucana* of 1569 are located the two Mexican conquest epics: Gabriel Lasso de la Vega's *Mexicana* of 1588 and Antonio de Saavedra Guzman's *El Peregrino Indiano* of 1599. While all four similarly narrate the Spanish imperial project, *Historia* and *Araucana* share relations of proximity: both narrate acts that take place after and far from the major undertakings of Cortés or Columbus, and both are published soon after the events they narrate.

10. The *Araucana* begins:

> No las Damas, amor, ni gentilezas
> de cavalleros canto enaborados
> Ni las muestras, regalso, y ternezas
> Mas el valor, los hechos, loas proezas
> De aquellos Españoles esforçados
> Que a la cerviz de Arauco no domada
> Pusieron duro yugo por la espada.
>
> (1.1–8)

11. For a discussion of "nation" as people and later as state, see "The Here, the Now," in *An Other Tongue,* 1–7.

12. The Spanish edition is titled *El Viaje que Hizo Antonio de Espejo;* the French edition, *Histoire des Terres Nouvellmente Descouvertes;* the English, *New Mexico, Otherwise, The Voyage of Anthony of Espejo.* Henry Wagner, *Spanish Southwest, 1542–1794* (New York: Arno, 1967), 150–7.

13. Erich Auerbach, *Mimesis: The Representation of Reality in Western Literature* (Princeton: Princeton U P, 1953). Robert Alter, *Partial Magic: The Novel as Self-Conscious Genre* (Berkeley and Los Angeles: U California P, 1975).

14. I do not argue that either Shakespeare or Cervantes invented irony. In many

ways what I choose to describe as novel in *Hamlet* and *Don Quixote* is traditional. Auerbach's noting Cervantes's dispersion of reality "in many individual adventures and sketches," for example, is found regularly in the epic. But what I do find novel in Shakespeare and in Cervantes is the degree to which irony is foregrounded as a prime trope for representation. To the irony that Auerbach envisions, that between character and story, and the irony I describe as that between reader and story, there can be added here the irony described by Bakhtin, that between author and character. This he sees most fully developed in the novels of Dostoyevsky and really present only in the genre of the novel. His views would support the general novelty of *Don Quixote,* especially when compared to drama, which Bakhtin aligned with poetry.

15. *Historia de la Nueva Mexico* is published in Madrid in 1610. I use the first publications for *Don Quixote* and *Hamlet,* that is, for part one of the *Quixote* and for the First Quarto of *Hamlet.*

16. I describe here only relative tendencies, the epic and the novelistic, and not the variety of individual poems and novels.

17. I am speaking of regional differences among Chicanos and not political differences, such as those that characterize the phenomenon of the Republican Hispanic. By northern New Mexicans I refer to those who live, roughly, north of Albuquerque and into southern Colorado. For various historical reasons, this region is markedly different than others, for example, than southern California or the valley of Texas.

18. This general comparison excludes West Texas, for El Paso is nearly as old as Santa Fe. It remained, however, closer to New Mexico and the West than to San Antonio and the center of population in the Rio Grande Valley.

19. While it seems logical to claim descendance from Spain, my point is that this is quite different from the perspectives of Chicanos in California or Texas or Mexicans. Generally, other Chicanos and Mexicans share the Mexican nationalist attitudes toward Spain, calling the Spanish, for example, "gachupines," after the Nahuatl meaning "he who kicks," because of the colonial acts toward the Indians.

20. Américo Paredes, *With His Pistol in His Hands: A Border Ballad and Its Hero* (Austin: U of Texas P, 1958).

21. For a discussion of the formulae for the corrido, see Arteaga, "The Chicano-Mexican Corrido," *Journal of Ethnic Studies* 13.2 (1985), 75–105.
    The California corrido, "Joaquín Murrieta," begins:

> Señors soy Mexicano
> pero compredo el inglés.
> Yo lo aprendí de mi hermano
> al derecho y al revés

> y a cualquier americano
> lo hago temblar a mis pies.

The Texan corrido, "Gregorio Cortez," begins:

> En el condado del Carmen
> miren lo que ha sucedido,
> murió el Cherife Mayor,
> quedando Román herido.

22. As David Lloyd says in "Adulteration and the Nation," "The national genius is to represent the nation in the double sense of depicting and embodying its spirit – or genius – as it is manifested in the changing forms of national life and history" (*An Other Tongue,* 53).
23. Gonzales, *I am Joaquín/Yo soy Joaquín* (New York: Bantam, 1972).
24. In a moment of self-consciousness, I pause here to ask whether I am doing what I ascribe to the New Mexican subject, that is, locating meaning today in a reading of the early modern epic. And that is part of my thesis: for even if I differentiate the New Mexican, I nevertheless argue that the *Historia de la Nueva Mexico* matters. My point, however, is that *how* it matters is quite different. I argue an essentially metonymic relation of the New Mexican to the *Historia,* it is, like land grant documents, local and historical, contiguous and continuous, with them. Were Sor Juana Inés de la Cruz to have read the *Historia,* as she might well have, I imagine that her relation to the masculine, hegemonic epic would be characterized by chiasmus. I imagine that Alurista would read the poem ironically. I read it dialogically.
25. Critics who have undertaken the delineation of poetics and the postmodern have looked at my poetry. For a discussion of the post-pomo poem, "Small Sea of Europe," and its contrast with more modernist contemporary poetry, see Majorie Perloff's "Postmodernism/Fin de Siècle: The Prospects for Openness in a Decade of Closure," in *Fin de Siècle Perspectives on Twentieth-Century Literature and Culture,* ed. Kathryne V. Lindberg, spec. issue of *Criticism* 35.2 (1993), 161–91.
26. In a letter of October 12, 1991, Gilles Deleuze wrote me, "Et pourtant quelque chose m'atteint profondément: vous faites partie de ces rares poètes qui savent dresser ou tailler dans leur langue une nouvelle langue. Des poèmes comme *Textos Vivos,* ou *Xronotop Xicano* m'enchantent. Une nouvelle langue dont les racines et les sources se feraient entendre, comme dans *Small Sea.*"

Index

十